THE GOSPEL OF THE FAMILY

Juan José Pérez-Soba and Stephan Kampowski

The Gospel
of the Family

Going Beyond Cardinal Kasper's
Proposal in the Debate on
Marriage, Civil Re-Marriage,
and Communion in the Church

Foreword by
George Cardinal Pell

Translated by
Michael J. Miller

IGNATIUS PRESS   SAN FRANCISCO

Cover design by Devin Schadt, Saint Louis Creative

© 2014 by Ignatius Press, San Francisco
All rights reserved
ISBN 978-1-58617-994-6
Library of Congress Control Number 2014911481
Printed in the United States of America ∞

CONTENTS

FOREWORD

This book is important for many reasons. A courteous, informed, and rigorous discussion, indeed debate, is needed especially for the coming months to defend the Christian and Catholic tradition of monogamous, indissoluble marriage—focusing on the central elements of the challenges facing marriage and the family, rather than being distracted into a counterproductive and futile search for short-term consolations.

The health of an organization can be gauged by observing the amount of time and energy devoted to the discussion of various topics. Healthy communities do not spend most of their energies on peripheral issues, and unfortunately the number of divorced and remarried Catholics who feel they should be allowed to receive Holy Communion is very small indeed.

The pressures for this change are centered mainly in some European churches, where churchgoing is low and an increasing number of divorcees are choosing not to remarry. The issue is seen by both friends and foes of the Catholic tradition as a symbol—a prize in the clash between what remains of Christendom in Europe and an aggressive neo-paganism. Every opponent of Christianity wants the Church to capitulate on this issue.

Both sides in this discussion appeal to Christian criteria, and everyone is dismayed by the amount of suffering caused to spouses and children by marriage breakups. What help can and should the Catholic Church offer?

Some see the primary task of the Church as providing lifeboats for those who have been shipwrecked by divorce. And lifeboats should be available for all, especially for those tragic innocent parties. But which way should the lifeboats be headed? Toward the rocks or the marshes, or to a safe port, which can only be reached with difficulty? Others see an even more important task for the Church in providing leadership and good maps to diminish the number of shipwrecks. Both tasks are necessary, but how are they best achieved?

The Christian understanding of mercy is central when we are talking about marriage and sexuality, forgiveness and Holy Communion, so not surprisingly, in this excellent volume the essential links between mercy and fidelity, between truth and grace in our Gospel teaching, are spelled out clearly and convincingly.

Mercy is different from most forms of tolerance, which is one of the more praiseworthy aspects of our pluralist societies. Some forms of tolerance define sin out of existence, but adult freedoms and inevitable differences need not be founded on a thoroughgoing relativism.

The indissolubility of marriage is one of the rich truths of divine revelation. It is no coincidence that monogamy and monotheism are found together in Judeo-Christianity. Lifelong marriage is not simply a burden but a jewel, a life-giving institution. When societies recognize this beauty and goodness, they regularly protect it with effective disciplinary measures. They realize that doctrine and pastoral practice cannot be contradictory, and that one cannot maintain the indissolubility of marriage by allowing the "remarried" to receive Holy Communion. Recognizing their inability to participate fully in the Eucharist is undoubtedly a sacrifice for believers, an imperfect but real form of sacrificial love.

Christianity and especially Catholicism constitute one historical reality, where the apostolic tradition of faith and morals, prayer and worship, is maintained. The doctrines of Christ are our cornerstone.

Interestingly, Jesus' hard teaching that "what therefore God has joined together, let no man put asunder" (Mt 19:6) follows not long after his insistence to Peter on the necessity of forgiveness (see Mt 18:21–35).

It is true that Jesus did not condemn the adulterous woman who was threatened with death by stoning, but he did not tell her to keep up her good work, to continue unchanged in her ways. He told her to sin no more (see Jn 8:1–11).

One insurmountable barrier for those advocating a new doctrinal and pastoral discipline for the reception of Holy Communion is the almost complete unanimity of two thousand years of Catholic history on this point. It is true that the Orthodox have a long-standing but different tradition, forced on them originally by their Byzantine emperors, but this has never been the Catholic practice.

One might claim that the penitential disciplines in the early centuries before the Council of Nicaea were too fierce as they argued whether those guilty of murder, adultery, or apostasy could be reconciled by the Church to their local communities only once—or not at all. They always acknowledged that God could forgive, even when the Church's ability to readmit sinners to the community was limited.

Such severity was the norm at a time when the Church was expanding in numbers, despite persecution. It can no more be ignored than the teachings of the Council of Trent or those of Saint John Paul II or Pope Benedict XVI on marriage can be ignored. Were the decisions that followed Henry VIII's divorce totally unnecessary?

This work contains some penetrating analyses of the cultural causes of family disintegration in today's pansexual culture. The point is well made that a correct diagnosis is more important than ever in an epidemic!

One claim is that divorce is the most important social revolution in modern times, and, without doubt, the crisis of marriage mirrors the crisis of faith and religious practice. Which is the chicken, and which is the egg?

As well as the long-standing intuition that a weakened faith means fewer children, I think it highly likely that the decision to have no children, or very few, itself results often in a serious weakening of faith. The influences run in both directions.

We are presently in a somewhat new situation, unparalleled since the days of the Second Vatican Council, where an increasing range of moral options are being canvassed publically, even by clerics. This brings benefits as an increased number of the formerly disinterested begin to discuss Christian claims, but pain and wounding are also inevitable.

Believers in the tradition, such as the authors of this volume, should be commended when they state their case calmly and charitably. We still have the best tunes.

We also need to work now to avoid a repetition of the aftermath of *Humanae vitae* in 1968. We should speak clearly, because the sooner the wounded, the lukewarm, and the outsiders realize that substantial doctrinal and pastoral changes are impossible, the more the hostile disappointment (which must follow the reassertion of doctrine) will be anticipated and dissipated.

George Cardinal Pell
Archbishop Emeritus of Melbourne and Sydney
Prefect of the Secretariat for the Economy
May 20, 2014

ABBREVIATIONS

DCE   Benedict XVI, Encyclical Letter *Deus caritas est*, December 25, 2005

EG   Francis, Apostolic Exhortation *Evangelii gaudium*, November 24, 2013

FC   John Paul II, Apostolic Exhortation *Familiaris consortio*, November 22, 1981

GS   Vatican Council II, Pastoral Constitution on the Church in the Modern World, *Gaudium et spes*, December 7, 1965

HV   Paul VI, Encyclical Letter *Humanae vitae*, July 25, 1968

LF   Francis, Encyclical Letter *Lumen fidei*, June 29, 2013

ST   Thomas Aquinas, *Summa theologica*

VS   John Paul II, Encyclical Letter *Veritatis splendor*, August 6, 1993

INTRODUCTION

As the Church has proclaimed at Vatican II, "The joy and hope, the grief and anguish of the men of our time, especially of those who are poor or afflicted in any way, are the joy and hope, the grief and anguish of the followers of Christ as well. Nothing that is genuinely human fails to find an echo in their hearts."[1] This is how the Church understands the divine mission that she must accomplish in the world. In particular, the task of the New Evangelization has made it clear to the ecclesial community, with renewed intensity, that the Christian family is an irreplaceable Christian witness by virtue of the profound reality that it contains.

Fifty years after the Council we can now describe as prophetic the interest that that assembly decided to take in the pastoral care of the family. In the meantime, it has become increasingly evident that this is not about just one of many human issues; rather, it is an essential part of divine revelation, precisely because the family hinges on love. A profound understanding of this is not a question of ideas, but rather it develops in the deeper relevance of the life of every family at the heart of a specific worldly setting.

One splendid light of this revelation is the Song of Solomon (Song of Songs), when the bride exclaims, in what is

<hr>

[1] Vatican II, Pastoral Constitution on the Church in the Modern World, *Gaudium et spes*, December 7, 1965, no. 1 (hereafter cited as *GS*).

the greatest expression of monogamous, faithful marriage: "My beloved is mine and I am his" (Song 2:16). This is the response to a *vocation to love* that springs from the perception of the Bridegroom's call (cf. Song 2:8), as Benedict XVI summarizes: "It is part of love's growth towards higher levels and inward purification that it now seeks to become definitive, and it does so in a twofold sense: both in the sense of exclusivity (this particular person alone) and in the sense of being 'for ever'."[2]

We can only welcome with great interest this initiative of a Synod on the family convoked by Pope Francis on the theme: "Pastoral Challenges to the Family in the Context of Evangelization". At the same time, we are completely in agreement with the way in which Walter Cardinal Kasper entitled his address to the Consistory of Cardinals on February 20, 2014: "The Gospel of the Family".[3] This gospel exists and is a light for the Church and for mankind.

Given Pope Francis' vigilance in maintaining the hierarchy of truths while transmitting the Gospel message,[4] we can confidently say that, presently, we have a clear awareness of the fact that the truth of the family, as the first and inescapable expression of the vocation of love, is part of its nucleus. The personal *integrity* that the family requires is the testimony that makes this love credible in the world.

---

[2] Benedict XVI, Encyclical Letter *Deus caritas est*, December 25, 2005, no. 6 (hereafter cited as *DCE*).

[3] Subsequently, the address was published in booklet form with the same title: Walter Cardinal Kasper, *The Gospel of the Family*, trans. William Madges (Mahwah, N.J.: Paulist Press, 2014). Hereafter, the booklet will be cited as *Gospel of the Family*.

[4] See Francis, Apostolic Exhortation *Evangelii gaudium*, November 24, 2013, no. 36 (hereafter cited as *EG*): "All revealed truths derive from the same divine source and are to be believed with the same faith, yet some of them are more important for giving direct expression to the heart of the Gospel."

This acknowledgment is the result of a profound renewal of our perception of the value of the revelation of spousal love in the Bible. This is what Benedict XVI highlights in *Deus caritas est*,[5] a concept repeated by Pope Francis in *Lumen fidei*, which presents spousal love in profound unity with the faith as something valuable for the common good of society.[6] Therefore we must say that we are addressing here one of the cardinal points of the faith. The specific characteristics of this conjugal love, including indissolubility, therefore, must be seen in light of the principal truths of Christianity.[7]

The introduction of marriage as a reality inscribed in the truth of creation, taken up by God to manifest his historical covenant with man, and definitively consecrated as a sacrament in the New Covenant of Christ, makes it uniquely valuable for understanding the human being as the "image" and "likeness" of God (see Gen 1:26) as well as the sacramental value of his love and his corporeality. This is what Saint John Paul II, the "pope of the family",[8] called an "adequate anthropology"—one capable of demonstrating its value as a fundamental dimension for the New Evangelization.[9] In our book we will follow in

[5] See *DCE* 5–11.

[6] See Francis, Encyclical Letter *Lumen fidei*, June 29, 2013, no. 52 (hereafter cited as *LF*).

[7] With this statement we address the following issue raised by Cardinal Kasper: "One must understand the doctrine of the indissolubility of marriage from [i.e., in terms of] the internal connection of the mysteries of faith" (*Gospel of the Family*, p. 44). Our argumentation will follow this line precisely.

[8] "Holy Mass and Rite of Canonization of Blesseds John XXIII and John Paul II: Homily of Pope Francis", April 27, 2014.

[9] The expression comes from John Paul II, Catechesis 13.2 (January 2, 1980), in his *Man and Woman He Created Them: A Theology of the Body*, trans. Michael Waldstein (Boston: Pauline Books and Media, 2006), p. 178; see also Catechesis 23.3 (April 2, 1980), in ibid., p. 220.

particular the teaching of the new saint, along the lines indicated by Pope Francis.

From this teaching we can deduce the intrinsic interrelatedness of creation, sin, and redemption that structures the Church's mission and, consequently, her pastoral ministry. This is how Cardinal Kasper intended to articulate his presentation of the theme, which can be summed up in the following psalm verse: "Mercy and faithfulness will meet" (Ps 85:10).

"Mercy and faithfulness" (or in some English translations, "truth") is in God an indissoluble binomial, so much so that it can be considered as the true revelation of him. The following verses of the psalm show us that the Lord is the one who makes it possible for these two things to meet on our earth, as seeds of salvation. This will be the principal light that will guide the reflections in this book.

Attempting to respond to the theme of the Synod in terms of the place where "mercy and truth meet" means, therefore, finding the light of a *truth of love* that we must examine more closely. We do this for the purpose of contributing to the open debate occasioned by the convocation of the Synod—a debate that we had better not try to cut short because of prejudices of any kind.

Therefore, let us take as our point of reference for this issue the booklet by Walter Cardinal Kasper, *The Gospel of the Family*, which contains important reflections, but, in our opinion, also contains significant inaccuracies. The goal of our contribution is to be able to develop the positive points, help clarify the ambiguous ones, and express the reasons why some statements seem to us seriously erroneous. But, above all, we intend to go beyond Cardinal Kasper's contribution to show in a simple, accessible way the extent to which it did not succeed in putting the gospel of the family at the center of its reflections, because it was focused on one point, which is important, certainly, but excessively narrow if made into an absolute.

The climate of dialogue that inspires our book therefore has something to do with the need to examine the questions in greater depth in a balanced way, starting with the dogmatic questions that cannot be taken for granted, which however, in recent years, have been the object of numerous studies. Consequently, although we will seek to clarify the terms of the question about reception of Holy Communion for the divorced and remarried, we will not concentrate exclusively on this aspect.[10]

In this sense, we were surprised to find in the German Cardinal's booklet a number of elements that are truly foreign to a healthy ecclesial debate—such as an expression that plainly sounds like a censure for those who adopt a certain position. It is incoherent with a text that is meant to open up a dialogue to use a type of argumentation that is alarming and excluding.[11] We hope that the Cardinal himself will qualify the import of his words, so that

[10] It is surprising that, even though Cardinal Kasper says that this is not the principal theme, 30 percent of his booklet deals directly with this topic. Practically no other pastoral directives appear, since he hardly mentions any of them in passing. Why neglect them when, in focusing on these questions, he ought to refer to a greater number of topics? Cf. *Gospel of the Family*, pp. 49–50: "Questions of marriage and family, under which the question of the divorced and remarried is indeed only one question—even though a pressing question—belong in the larger context of the question of how people can find happiness and fulfillment in their lives." Why does he not take up again the questions that appear in the introduction (pp. 1–5), or go further in his discussion about the domestic church (i.e., the family)? (pp. 20–25).

[11] The reader can judge for himself; see *Gospel of the Family*, p. 47: "In this matter, there are great expectations in the Church. Beyond a doubt, we cannot fulfill all expectations. But it would cause a terrible disappointment if we would only repeat the answers that supposedly have always been given. As

everyone can express himself with complete freedom in the next Synod.

All this compels us to make sure that in all these questions we bring to light especially those things which do not appear in Cardinal Kasper's book but which can be the source of a more open and fruitful dialogue with a view to the Synod, without reducing our discussion to a single question.

We will begin therefore by addressing the cultural challenge as the fundamental key to understanding the role of the family in the dialogue between the Church and the world; this is a pivotal point if we are to avoid the many misunderstandings of the gospel of the family. Next, we will identify the centrality of the family in the Christian proclamation, adopting the perspective of a God who reveals himself as mercy, an approach that we will complete in the third chapter with a brief review of some patristic texts that teach the way in which the primitive Church experienced the question. Then we will go on to analyze the matter from the more contemporary moral perspective, considering therefore the construction of the moral subject by means of his actions, and we will conclude by outlining what could be "adequate pastoral care", given the challenges of our time.[12]

---

witnesses of hope, we [must] not allow ourselves to be led by a hermeneutic of fear. Some courage and above all biblical candor (*parrhesia*) are necessary. If we don't want that, then we should not hold a synod on this topic, because then the situation would be worse afterwards than before."

[12]We shared the work throughout, and in its entirety the book should be considered as the work of both authors. In any case, the composition of the first and fourth chapters was entrusted to Prof. Stephan Kampowski, while the second, third, and fifth chapters were composed by Prof. Juan José Pérez-Soba.

We hope that the simple statement of the themes and the sequence thereof may bring the reader to appreciate this perspective of a logic of love, which ought to imbue all the actions of the Church.

Announcing the Gospel of the Family
in a Sex-Saturated Culture

1.1. The Beauty of the Gospel of the Family:
Love and Human Sexuality

"We may not limit the discussion [of the gospel of the family] to the situation of the divorced and remarried or to many other difficult pastoral situations that have not been mentioned in this context. We must begin positively, discovering and proclaiming again the gospel of the family in its total beauty. Truth persuades by means of its beauty."[1] These indeed profound words by Walter Cardinal Kasper are in complete consonance with Pope Francis' desire—expressed before the Extraordinary Consistory that was to be addressed by the Cardinal—to avoid "falling into 'casuistry'", but rather to "acknowledge how beautiful, true and good it is to start a family, to be a family today; and how indispensable the family is for the life of the world and for the future of humanity".[2] In this present chapter, we will seek to follow this approach, examining where it is that the compelling and convincing beauty of the gospel of the family can be found. We will also examine the

[1] *Gospel of the Family*, pp. 33–34.
[2] "Extraordinary Consistory: Address of Pope Francis", February 20, 2014.

obstacles that a proclamation of this good news encounters in today's cultural context and consider possible ways of confronting and overcoming them.

Where is, then, the beauty of the Christian vision of the family? What is *good* and what is *new* about the good news that Christ and his Church have proclaimed about marriage and the family? When the Gospel "hit" the ancient Greco-Roman world, it brought with it a true novelty, profoundly challenging that culture in ways that are analogous to our own contemporary situation.[3] To see the novelty of the Gospel, let us have a look at the advice the ancient Roman writer Lucretius gave to young men in love:

> Though she thou lovest now be far away,
> Yet idol-images of her are near
> And the sweet name is floating in thy ear.
> But it behooves to flee those images;
> And scare afar whatever feeds thy love;
> And turn elsewhere thy mind; and vent the sperm,
> Within thee gathered, into sundry bodies,
> Nor, with thy thoughts still busied with one love,
> Keep it for one delight, and so store up
> Care for thyself and pain inevitable.
>
> . . . .
>
> For the delights of Venus, verily,
> Are more unmixed for mortals sane-of-soul
> Than for those sick-at-heart with love-pining.[4]

---

[3] Cf. *Gospel of the Family*, pp. 2–3: "The current situation of the Church is not unique. Even the church of the first centuries was confronted with concepts and models of marriage and family that were different from that which Jesus preached, which was quite new, both for Jews as well as for the Greeks and Romans."

[4] Lucretius, *On the Nature of Things*, Book IV.

What does Lucretius say here on the nature of human love? In beautiful, truly poetic words, he quite prosaically says that a man should sleep with many different women and not get attached to one, lest he suffer from his affection for her. Besides, he suggests that the pleasure of intercourse is purer when one is not distracted by being in love. It thus seems that for him, sexual relations have little or nothing to do with love.

A very similar separation of sexuality from love can be found at the root of the so-called sexual revolution, a term that has usually come to be associated with the events of the 1960s, but which has one of its ideological roots in the highly influential book *The Sexual Revolution* written by the Austrian psychoanalyst Wilhelm Reich (first published in German in 1936 under the title *Sexualität im Kulturkampf: Zur sozialistischen Umstrukturierung des Menschen* [*Sexuality in the Culture War: Toward the Socialistic Restructuring of Man*]).[5] According to Reich, "medical experience with sexuality teaches us that sexual repression causes disease, perversions, or lasciviousness."[6] For him, "abstinence is dangerous and absolutely deleterious to health",[7] while sexual practice serves as therapy; sexual pleasure leads to health and happiness: "Sexual energy is the biological energy which, in the psyche, determines the character of human feeling and thinking."[8] Then he proceeds, "The

[5] Wilhelm Reich, *The Sexual Revolution*, trans. Therese Pol (New York: Farrar, Straus and Giroux, 1974). First published in English in 1945 by the Orgone Institute Press in New York. The original German edition was first published as *Sexualität im Kulturkampf: Zur sozialistischen Umstrukturierung des Menschen* (Kopenhagen: Sexpol-Verlag, 1936).

[6] Reich, *Sexual Revolution*, p. 66.

[7] Ibid., 108.

[8] Ibid., xxiii.

core of happiness in life is sexual happiness."[9] As modern as this approach purports to be, it cannot be denied that it strongly resembles Lucretius' rather ancient view: what matters for sexuality is not love but the sexual pleasure or the "sexual energy".

Both for Lucretius in ancient Rome and for Reich in the modern West, the other is only of secondary importance when it comes to sexual relations. In both cases sexual activity is completely severed from love. For Reich in particular, this is so because human persons must necessarily be sexually active. If they abstain, they become sick. The need to have sex would then be similar to the need to have food. One can go without it only for so long. If this were so, then sexual activity would be removed from the realm of the person's freedom and responsibility. If we must of necessity engage in sexual encounters—whether it is a necessity of impulse or a requirement of mental or physical health—a sexual act could hardly be called an encounter of love. If in the field of human sexuality self-control and abstinence were not possible, sexual acts could scarcely make the claim to be expressions of love, since love by nature is something that is entrusted to our freedom.

What is proper to love is the logic of the gift: it has to be freely given and freely received. What would a wife think of her husband who wakes her up at three o'clock in the morning and asks her for relations because he suddenly feels a strong sexual urge? How could such a sexual act be an act of love? How would a sexual encounter then be different from the much more mundane and trivial ways in which all human beings have to relieve themselves several

[9] Ibid., xxvi.

times each day? Exclusivity and permanence in a relation between a man and a woman would be impossible. If one of the partners were to go on a business trip, neither could expect of the other to abstain from sexual relations during the time of absence, any more than they could expect each other to abstain from eating and drinking all those days. If, as Reich has it, persons really had to satisfy every urge that befalls them so as not to develop serious mental conditions, then exclusive and lasting relationships would indeed be serious health hazards, as he himself concluded.

We may wonder, however, whether this perspective is beautiful. It would seem that it is part of erotic love's very nature to desire exclusivity and durability. Love seems to want to say, "You are my one and only: I am all yours and you are all mine. I give you all of myself—exclusively and for the rest of my life." It is here that the Gospel brought in a true novelty in the ancient world, and it does so again today; the field of human sexuality, that is, the realm that touches on our sexual differentiation, can be redeemed and raised up—it no longer needs to be the battlefield of mutual exploitation, domination, and seduction. Jesus offers us a new power: sexuality can have something to do with love. Before the author of Ephesians exhorts the wives to be "subject to" their "husbands, as to the Lord" (Eph 5:22), he tells husbands and wives to be "subject to one another out of reverence for Christ" (Eph 5:21) and then continues to call on the husbands to love their wives "as Christ loved the Church and gave himself up for her" (Eph 5:25).

This, now, is truly a beautiful love and is only possible as such if the "forever" is possible. The indissolubility of marriage together with sexual exclusivity is not an additional heavy burden placed on Christian spouses. Rather, it is a quintessential part of the meaning of true love and is given to the followers of Jesus as a new possibility. As Cardinal Kasper rightly puts it, the teaching concerning the indissoluble bond of marriage "is good news, that is, definitive solace and a pledge that continues to be valid".[10] The indissolubility of marriage and sexual exclusivity are good news; it is divorce and unfaithfulness that are the bad news. Divorce and unfaithfulness derive from the "hardness of heart" (Mt 19:8). Jesus says, "What therefore God has joined together, let no man put asunder" (Mt 19:6). Here we must remember that he is the Word by which God the Father created the universe; if he says it, then it will be. Thus, by giving the command to "let no man put asunder", he also provides the *possibility* of lifelong fidelity, and with this a gift for which our hearts yearn. In the novel *Per sempre* (*Forever*) by Susanna Tamaro, the protagonist is asked by his wife: "Does the 'forever' exist?" The answer he gives her is, "The *only* thing that exists is the 'forever'."[11] True love wants to say "forever".

In a magnificent sonnet, William Shakespeare expresses the intimate connection between love and the "forever" in the following moving terms:

> Let me not to the marriage of true minds
> Admit impediments. Love is not love
> Which alters when it alteration finds,
> Or bends with the remover to remove:
> O no! it is an ever-fixed mark
> That looks on tempests and is never shaken;

[10] *Gospel of the Family*, p. 16.
[11] Susanna Tamaro, *Per sempre* (Milan: Giunti, 2011), p. 12.

It is the star to every wandering bark,
Whose worth's unknown, although his height be
    taken.
Love's not Time's fool, though rosy lips and
    cheeks
Within his bending sickle's compass come:
Love alters not with his brief hours and weeks,
But bears it out even to the edge of doom.
If this be error and upon me proved,
I never writ, nor no man ever loved.[12]

The "forever" is *good* news. Anyone who has ever loved would want this love to last forever. The question, then, is another: it is not whether we want it, but whether we think it possible. And here the good *news* comes in. The forever is a true novelty brought by Christ, a new possibility that corresponds to the deepest yearnings of our hearts. This is no doubt countercultural. As Pope Francis puts it, today's culture is a "culture of the temporary" or a "culture of the provisory".[13] He exhorts couples not to let themselves be overcome by this cultural context but to found their homes "on the rock of true love, the love that comes from God".[14] In a very suggestive image the Pope insists that Christ is quite capable of multiplying the couple's love just as he multiplied the loaves of bread, giving it to them "fresh and good each day".[15]

In light of the fact that the possibility of the "forever" is an essential part of what is good and new about the

---

[12] William Shakespeare, Sonnet 116.
[13] "Address of Pope Francis to Engaged Couples Preparing for Marriage", February 14, 2014.
[14] Ibid.
[15] Ibid.

good news, it is not entirely clear what Cardinal Kasper refers to when, in the context of discussing the question of admitting the divorced and remarried to Communion, he asks for "a renewed pastoral spirituality that takes leave of a narrow, legalistic view and an unchristian rigorism that places on people intolerable burdens that we clerics ourselves do not want to bear and also could not bear (see Matt 23:4)".[16] What are the "intolerable burdens" referred to here? Could one burden be the indissolubility of marriage? This would be inconsistent with what he says elsewhere, when he refers to the indissoluble bond as "good news",[17] and when he insists on not wanting to put marital indissolubility into question.[18]

It seems more likely that the intolerable burden ultimately amounts to being sexually exclusive. This, at least, is the highly plausible way in which Carlo Cardinal Caffarra interprets Cardinal Kasper's proposal. It is impossible to deny that by admitting some of the divorced and remarried to Communion—even if these couples performed prior acts of penance that however fall short of a qualitative change in their state of life—the Church would "grant a judgment of legitimacy to the second union".[19] But this second union cannot be a second

---

[16] *Gospel of the Family*, p. 50.

[17] Ibid., p. 16.

[18] Cf. ibid., p. 43: "No one questions the indissolubility of a sacramental marriage that was contracted and consummated (*ratum* and *consumatum*)."

[19] Carlo Caffarra, interview, "Da Bologna con amore: fermatevi" [*From Bologna with Love: Stop It*], *Il Foglio*, March 14, 2014. An English translation of the whole interview, unfortunately containing significant imprecisions, is available at http://www.zenit.org/en/articles/cardinal-caffarra-expresses-serious-concerns-about-family-synod-debates#. The present, more accurate English translation, is taken from an excerpt reproduced in *Crisis Magaine* at http://www.crisismagazine.com/2014/a-rival-good-to-gods-cardinal-kaspers-divorce-proposal.

marriage, contemporaneous to the first, "considering that bigamy goes against the word of the Lord".[20] Given that Cardinal Kasper explicitly upholds the indissolubility of marriage, and given that he would hardly want to propose that a person could live in two valid and indissoluble marriages at the same time, his solution effectively seems to suggest that "the first matrimony remains, but that there is also a second kind of cohabitation that the Church legitimizes."[21] For Cardinal Caffarra the most serious implication of this proposal is the following: "It is, therefore, an extramarital exercise of human sexuality that the Church legitimizes. But with this, the foundational pillar of the Church's doctrine on sexuality is negated"—that pillar being the Church's insistence that the only proper setting for the exercise of sexuality is the context of conjugal love.

It seems that Cardinal Kasper overlooks the connection between indissolubility and sexual exclusivity. In any case if, when speaking about "intolerable burdens", he intends either the indissolubility of marriage or the requirement of sexual exclusivity, then the Bible passage that comes to mind in this context will not be Matthew 23:4 ("They bind heavy burdens, hard to bear"), but rather Matthew 19:10, where we learn about the disciples' astonishment at Jesus' teaching on marriage: "If such is the case of a man with his wife, it is not expedient to marry."

Again, the requirements of the indissolubility of marriage and of the sexual exclusivity of the spouses are not heavy burdens placed on the marriage partners by Christ or his Church. They are the requirements of love itself.

[20] Ibid.
[21] Ibid.

Anyone who has ever "fallen in love" will be able to verify this in his own experience. The issue is that we also "fall out of love". The romance, when the lovers promise the stars to each other, lasts but for a moment. The good news is that this initial moment, the promise of eros, can find its fulfillment in agape.[22] While it is certainly true that an individual is not a "workhorse" and while there is a way in which we can say that we are "created for the Sabbath"[23]—inasmuch as the Sabbath rest is a "rest in the Lord" in remembrance, praise, and thanksgiving[24]—it is also true that there is a sense in which we are created to work constantly, namely, inasmuch as we are created to love. Love requires constant labor. As Francesco Botturi puts it, "[Love] is the work of freedom; it requires labor and has the dimension of duration. To love means wanting to love, that is, freely to assume the affective intentionality that being in love offers spontaneously."[25] In this sense also Erich Fromm can say, "The essence of love is to 'labor' for something and 'to make something grow'.... Love and labor are inseparable. One loves that for which one labors, and one labors for that which one loves."[26] This labor of love is itself God's gift to us. By giving us his grace, God does not simply cover our ugliness. Rather, he transforms us from within, giving us the gift of a new action.[27] The

[22] Cf. DCE 3–8.

[23] Gospel of the Family, p. 9.

[24] Cf. John Paul II, Apostolic Letter Dies Domini, May 31, 1998, no. 16.

[25] Francesco Botturi, La generazione del bene. Gratuità ed esperienza morale (Milano: Vita and Pensiero, 2009), p. 222 (translation our own).

[26] Erich Fromm, The Essence of Love (New York: Harper and Row, 1956), p. 27.

[27] Cf. Livio Melina, The Epiphany of Love: Toward a Theological Understanding of Human Action (Grand Rapids, Mich.: Eerdmans, 2010), p. 115: "Grace is understood as an interior dynamic principle, as the gift of a new way of acting."

good news is, the promise of love can be fulfilled. Love can be lasting and faithful.

Here is indeed the cornerstone of the Church's teaching on human sexuality and its relation to love. She teaches that sexual acts can be acts of true love only if they are conjugal acts, that is, if they are accomplished by a man and a woman who have publically committed their lives to each other, who have promised each other fidelity and sexual exclusivity, and who are open to the generation of new life. She derives this teaching from the very nature of conjugal love as human, total, faithful and exclusive, and fruitful.[28] But as we have said before, it is possible for sexual acts to be acts of conjugal love only if abstinence is possible. If Reich is right and abstinence leads to neuroses, then no one in his right mind should exchange marital vows. If abstinence, whether temporal or total, were impossible, then sexual acts could never be expressions of conjugal love, since they would be accomplished under the urge of necessity. Sexual exclusivity would also be impossible, since there will always be times in which the marriage partners *have to* abstain, even if just because the wife has a headache, not to mention more serious and perhaps even permanent health reasons. If someone *has to* have sex and cannot go to his spouse, because she is ill-disposed, then he has to go somewhere else, just as he still has to eat, even if he cannot eat with her. In this case, love would be asking for an exclusiveness that sex cannot give. Sex and love would be in two entirely different spheres. The fact that they belong together is the good news of the Gospel, and they can go together because abstinence is possible. This is perhaps the

---

[28] Cf. Paul VI, Encyclical Letter *Humanae vitae*, July 25, 1968, no. 9 (hereafter cited as *HV*).

Church's major challenge to ancient as well as contemporary culture. It is a completely different anthropology than the one that is being advocated in today's society, which has bought into Reich's fundamental premise.

1.2. Is Abstinence Thinkable? *Familiaris consortio* and *Sacramentum caritatis* on the Divorced and Civilly Remarried

Having seen how important the possibility of abstinence is if sexuality is meant to have anything to do with love, we must note one of the most curious facts about Cardinal Kasper's speech before the Consistory. Its fifth part is about the question of admitting the divorced and civilly remarried to Communion. He argues that John Paul II and Benedict XVI in *Familiaris consortio* and *Sacramentum caritatis*, respectively, have hinted at possible solutions to the problem, listing two of these in particular: the high incidence of invalid marriages and the possibility of spiritual communion.[29] Why not simplify the annulment process, so as to make it easier for the divorced and civilly remarried who are convinced that their first marriage was invalid, to regularize their canonical situation?[30] If the divorced and

[29] Cf. *Gospel of the Family*, pp. 28–33; John Paul II, Apostolic Exhortation *Familiaris consortio*, November 22, 1981, no. 84 (hereafter cited as *FC*); and Benedict XVI, Post-Synodal Apostolic Exhortation *Sacramentum caritatis*, February 22, 2007, no. 29.

[30] There is an evident tension, if not an outright contradiction, between Cardinal Kasper's affirmation that "it would be mistaken to seek the resolution of the problem in a generous expansion of the annulment process" (*Gospel of the Family*, p. 29) and his suggestion to search for "more pastoral and spiritual procedures" in this context, possibly having the bishop "entrust this task to a priest

civilly remarried can receive spiritual "extra-sacramental" communion, why can they not receive sacramental Communion?[31] Would not a development of doctrine toward a toleration of their lifestyle be thinkable?[32] Much can be said about Cardinal Kasper's suggestions here, and we will do so in due course. In the present discussion, however, we will focus on what he is *not* saying; we will discuss a significant silence.

The fact is that, for some reason or other, he is not giving us the complete state of the debate here before presenting his new solutions. He cites *Familiaris consortio* (no. 84) and *Sacramentum caritatis* (no. 29) to emphasize the new, more merciful tone the Church has found when speaking about the divorced and remarried, arguing that they "hint at"[33] solutions such as annulment and spiritual communion. However, the one practice both passages do not simply "hint at", but clearly profess, is a solution the Cardinal does not so much as mention. It has two elements. The first is to point to the general "obligation to separate".[34] In the paragraphs under discussion, both documents, however, acknowledge that there can be cases in which this obligation cannot be fulfilled without violating

---

with spiritual and pastoral experience as a penitentiary or episcopal vicar" (ibid., p. 28), which in practice amounts precisely to what the Cardinal professes to be a mistaken resolution, namely, "a generous expansion of the annulment process". We will discuss this point in more depth in a later chapter.

[31] Ibid., p. 30.

[32] Cf. ibid., p. 27: "Is not a further development possible with regard to our issue too—a development that does not repeal the binding faith tradition, but carries forward and deepens more recent traditions?"

[33] Cf. ibid., pp. 27–28: "I will limit myself to two situations, for which solutions are already mentioned [German: *angedeutet*, 'hinted at'] in the official documents."

[34] Cf. *FC* 84.

serious commitments already undertaken, in particular those to children born of the second union. In this case, the practice called for by both documents stays short of separation.

As to the essential obligation to *abandon* a civil union, it is noteworthy that Cardinal Kasper actually does more than simply not mention it; he in fact proposes the exact opposite, namely, that it could be necessary to *enter* one, which then may be experienced as "a virtual gift from heaven": "However, many deserted partners, for the sake of the children, are dependent upon a new partnership and a civil marriage, which they cannot again quit without new guilt."[35] It is true that *Familiaris consortio* acknowledges that some may seek a second union "for the sake of the children's upbringing" (no. 84). The document makes it clear, however, that even such a humanly understandable motivation does not justify the violation of one's marital promises. Besides, it seems to be not only a matter of the classical fairytale but also of statistically observable fact that the relationship between stepparents and stepchildren is often far from harmonious. Thus, there is clear evidence that stepchildren are at a higher risk of being abused than other children.[36] Put differently, it is not certain that it is better

[35] *Gospel of the Family*, p. 26. That this is not a slip of the pen can be seen by the fact that the Cardinal repeats the same idea in a different place: "If, let's say, a woman was abandoned due to no fault of her own and, *for the sake of her children, she needs a husband or a father,* and she honestly endeavors to live a Christian life in the second, civilly contracted marriage and family, and she raises her children as Christians and is involved in her parish in exemplary fashion (which is very often the case), then this too belongs to the objective situation" (p. 45; emphasis added).

[36] See, for instance, N. Zoe Hilton, Grant T. Harris, and Marnie E. Rice, "The Step-Father Effect in Child Abuse: Comparing Discriminative Parental Solicitude and Antisociality", *Psychology of Violence*, advance online

for the children of an unjustly abandoned partner to grow up with a stepparent rather than with just one parent. It is at least not as obvious as the Cardinal implies that it is. In any case, to suggest that an abandoned partner could be under moral necessity[37] to enter a second union, a union that could be seen as a gift from heaven, is indeed a novelty that is literally reversing previous Magisterial teaching.

But now let us take the case of the divorced and civilly remarried who indeed share a serious common commitment that makes their separation morally impossible, a commitment such as one to children born of this union.[38] Here, too, *Familiaris consortio* (no. 84) and *Sacramentum caritatis* (no. 29) have spoken explicitly. Both documents

---

publication, April 2014, http://dx.doi.org/10.1037/a0035189; Vivian A. Weekes-Shackelford and Todd K. Shackelford, "Methods of Filicide: Stepparents and Genetic Parents Kill Differently", *Violence and Victims* 19 (2004): 75–81.

[37] That is, moral necessity inasmuch as it is for the sake of what is argued to be for the good of the children, which the abandoned partner feels himself to be morally obliged to assure.

[38] *Familiaris consortio* (no. 84) speaks of children twice, in what can be argued to be two different situations. The first context is this: referring to the divorced and civilly remarried "who have entered into a second union for the sake of the children's upbringing", John Paul II seems to have in mind the children born to validly married spouses, one of whom abandons his partner and their common children. As we immediately learn a few lines down, these children *are not* a justifying motive for the abandoned partner to enter a new union, however humanly understandable this motive might be and however much pastors of souls are called to keep in mind the alleviating (though not justifying) circumstances. Secondly, *Familiaris consortio*, in the same numbered paragraph, mentions the situation in which "for serious reasons such as, for example, the children's upbringing, a man and a woman cannot satisfy the obligation to separate". These would seem to be children born of a civil union, who *are* a justifying motive for the civil partners (father and mother of the same children) to continue their cohabitation, though not their intimate relations. While in the latter case there is a moral impossibility for the civil partners to separate, in the former case there is no moral impossibility for the abandoned partner to stay as he is. Cardinal Kasper gives the impression of merging the two cases.

make it clear that these people are not in a situation where they *have to* sin. There is a feasible way out. In *Familiaris consortio* we read:

> Reconciliation in the sacrament of penance, which would open the way to the Eucharist, can only be granted to those who, repenting of having broken the sign of the covenant and of fidelity to Christ, are sincerely ready to undertake a way of life that is no longer in contradiction to the indissolubility of marriage.
>
> This means, in practice, that when, for serious reasons such as, for example, the children's upbringing, a man and a woman cannot satisfy the obligation to separate, they "take on themselves the duty to live in complete continence, that is, by abstinence from the acts proper to married couples". (no. 84)

In *Sacramentum caritatis* Benedict XVI reiterates the same idea when he writes about the divorced and remarried:

> Where the nullity of the marriage bond is not declared and objective circumstances make it impossible to cease cohabitation, the Church encourages these members of the faithful to commit themselves to living their relationship in fidelity to the demands of God's law, as friends, as brother and sister; in this way they will be able to return to the table of the Eucharist. (no. 29)

To our minds it is of utmost importance to emphasize that already today the Church's practice indicates a condition under which cohabiting divorced and civilly remarried couples can receive the Eucharist. The divorced and civilly remarried can receive the Eucharist (and the other sacraments) even if they share the same home—namely, once they renounce sharing the same bed.

We wonder why Cardinal Kasper does not mention this solution. It is proposed in documents and paragraphs that he is citing. It is hence unlikely that he is not familiar with it. Could this solution be so much out of the question for him that he does not even consider it worth mentioning? But is it really out of the question?[39] Are not Saint John Paul II and Benedict XVI presenting us with a highly positive view of the person as a being who is capable of self-possession and self-dominion, who is able to integrate his sexuality into the field of personal responsibility and is, as such, also able to abstain from sexual relations, in particular when he receives the grace of the Holy Spirit, the New Law, as a new principle of action?[40]

"Truth persuades by means of its beauty."[41] If truth is indeed beautiful, would this not also mean that beauty is a heuristic principle of truth, just as ugliness is an indicator for falsehood? Is it not the more beautiful position to say that human sexuality is a field in which responsible behavior is possible, a field that does not fall out of the sphere of

[39] Only after having been explicitly asked about this question by the journalists conducting an interview with him for the *Commonweal* magazine, Cardinal Kasper finally addresses the issue, openly dismissing it as not feasible, revealing a rather pessimistic view of the ordinary faithful: "To live together as brother and sister? Of course I have high respect for those who are doing this. But it's a heroic act, and heroism is not for the average Christian" (Matthew Boudway and Grant Gallicho, "Merciful God, Merciful Church: An Interview with Cardinal Walter Kasper", May 7, 2014, https://www.commonwealmagazine.org/kasper-interview-popefrancis-vatican).

[40] Cf. *Gospel of the Family*, p. 4, where he explicitly refers to Saint Thomas Aquinas' treatment of the New Law of the Gospel in *Summa theologica*, I–II, q. 106 (hereafter cited as *ST*).

[41] *Gospel of the Family*, pp. 33–34.

self-possession and self-dominion,[42] a field in which love can be truly expressed? Is not the position advocated by our contemporary pansexualistic culture much less beautiful, if not to say ugly, namely, the position that says that abstinence is not possible, and that effectively suggests that the only relevant difference between the way humans and irrational animals live out their sexual urges lies in the fact that humans know how to use a condom?

A particularly stark example for this inhuman way of looking at sexuality can be found in the German government's campaign to fight venereal disease, an objective that is, as such, of course laudable. Yet the result is that German citizens have to see their country plastered with billboards adorned with condoms and the more or less subtle suggestions of all kinds of sexual practices. The morale that is being proposed is this: anything goes, inside and outside of marriage, between people of the same or of the opposite sex, making use of any opening of the body whatsoever. Between consenting adults there is just one commandment: "Use a condom." What is the German government teaching the children of its generation? Is this not a highly pessimistic view of the human person and of his sexuality? Marital faithfulness as a path to stop the spread of venereal disease does not seem to be an option. There is no way people can govern their sexual behavior. Premarital abstinence as a way to avoid teenage pregnancies? This too

[42] These ideas, of course, were very dear to Karol Wojtyła, expressed particularly in his *Love and Responsibility* (New York: Farrar, Straus and Giroux, 1981); in his profound and concise defense of *Humanae vitae* in "La visione antropologica della *Humanae vitae*", *Lateranum* 44 (1978): 125–45; and, of course, when writing as pope, in his Wednesday Catechesis on human love published as *Man and Woman He Created Them: A Theology of the Body* (Boston: Pauline Books and Media, 2006).

would have to appear entirely absurd in a society that celebrates the condom as the redemption of human sexuality, a tendency evidently present not only in Germany but in most of Western societies. What could be more fatal for the Church's proclamation of the gospel of the family in such a context than even remotely to give the impression that she herself does not believe that human sexuality is a sphere governed by the requirements of love, that she herself does not believe that if love requires abstinence, abstinence will be possible?

The greatest of the pastoral challenges to the family in the context of evangelization, then, is this: how are we to proclaim the gospel of the family in a pansexualistic culture? This is a culture that has bought into the fundamental premises of the sexual revolution, as proposed, for instance, by Wilhelm Reich: life's energy is sexual energy; sex is for recreation not for procreation; abstinence from sex is as impossible as abstinence from food and drink—people need sex as they need bread and water. It is no wonder, then, that people negotiate sex as they negotiate all other necessities of life, that they sell and buy sex like commodities. The Church has always resisted this premise, proclaiming, as stated earlier, that sex is for conjugal love, a love that is human, total, exclusive, lasting, and fruitful.[43] Of course, to the mind of many of our contemporaries, the Church simply teaches that sex is for procreation. Certainly she insists on the fact that sex and babies have to be thought together, and yet, there is more to it. A man who goes in to a prostitute with the explicit intention of getting her pregnant still commits a sin, according to the

[43] See *HV* 9.

teaching of the Church. What the Church is really teaching and has always taught is that the only proper context
for the exercise of human sexuality is the context of conjugal love. The argument of *Humanae vitae* is that it is conjugal love itself that requires each and every marriage act to
be open to the procreation of new life.[44] In other words,
a sexual encounter in which the spouses deliberately render themselves sterile cannot be called an act of conjugal love, which is why it is sinful.[45] Sex is for conjugal
love. Outside of the context of this love it neither attains
its truth nor its beauty. Sex can only be for love if we
are free in its exercise, that is, if we are free periodically
or even permanently to abstain, given that there will be
circumstances—a spouse's temporary absence for a business trip, his ill health, a high number of children—under
which abstinence becomes love's requirement. Abstaining
may be difficult and demanding; we may fall and be called
to rise again, but in principle abstaining is possible.

If we, as children of the Church, do not believe that it
is humanly possible, medically healthy, or socially advis-
able to restrict the exercise of human sexuality to conjugal
acts (i.e., freely chosen acts of sexual intimacy performed
by a man and a woman who have publicly pledged lifelong fidelity and sexual exclusivity to each other and who
preserve an openness to the procreation of new life),
then we should stop altogether speaking about matters

---

[44] *HV* 11.

[45] See the excellent treatment of this topic by Martin Rhonheimer in "Sexuality and Responsibility: Contraception as an Ethical Problem", *Ethics of
Procreation and the Defense of Human Life: Contraception, Artificial Fertilization,
and Abortion* (Washington, D.C.: Catholic University of America Press, 2010),
pp. 33–132.

concerning human sexuality, the family, human life, and human dignity. Most everything the Church says on these issues stands or falls with this principal teaching on the adequate place of human sexuality. The Church says that it belongs to the dignity of the human person to be conceived in an act of conjugal love, to be the incarnation of the love between husband and wife, not the product of people's will to power and dominion. If it is impossible to restrict the exercise of human sexuality to acts accomplished within the conjugal union, then no child could be said to have a right to be born of such a union. No injustice would be done to a child born to a mother who does not even remember its father's name, and no injustice would be done to a child born as a result of the powers of technology, manufactured as the product of a domineering will. If the origin of human life is not a gift, then why not rid oneself of it when it is no longer convenient? If I have not received myself as a gift, but have been forced into being by the manipulating will of my parent(s), why not put an end to my life when I see fit? Why should society not put an end to the life of its citizens when it sees fit?

1.3. The Family and the Evangelization of a Culture

The topic of the upcoming Synod is "The Pastoral Challenges to the Family in the Context of Evangelization". One could approach this theme by considering to what extent the Church's teaching on human sexuality, marriage, and family presents itself as an obstacle to evangelization. Would the Church's teaching not become more attractive if it became more accommodating, for instance, by tolerating certain types of sexual activity outside of marriage, such as in the case of the divorced and civilly remarried? But then, as Cardinal Caffarra acutely observes, why not also tolerate the premarital or homosexual exercise of one's sexuality?[46] By taking away the stumbling block on which is written that sex is for conjugal love, we will also remove the cornerstone. We should then leave the talk about sexuality to sexologists, and the debate about marriage and family to psychologists and sociologists.

Would the cause of evangelization be served in this way? It seems that it would not. Let us take the example of a good number of churches and ecclesial realities from the Anglican and Protestant traditions. It is not an expression of disrespect but simply a statement of fact that many of them have, for all intents and purposes, renounced insisting on the morally more demanding aspects of the gospel of the family. Contraception, artificial procreation, divorce and remarriage, premarital sex, the blessing of homosexual unions—all this is largely being tolerated, if not outright promoted, by many of these institutions. And yet, has this tolerance led to a spiritual revival of the Church of England? Are the German Lutherans thriving? Is there a new springtime for liberal American Presbyterians? The sociological data would seem to imply the contrary. In fact, the American sociologist Mary Eberstadt, in her highly instructive *How the West Really Lost God*, suggests that the more mainline liberal Protestant and Anglican churches are declining in attendance, membership, and general vitality. To her mind, these institutions are committing what she calls an "assisted religious suicide"

---

[46] See Caffarra, "Da Bologna con amore" [From Bologna with Love].

that is due to their failure to take the family seriously: "In their efforts to reach out to individuals who wanted a softening of Christian doctrine, the churches inadvertently appear to have failed to protect their base: thriving families whose members would then go on to reproduce both literally and in the figurative sense of handing down their religion."[47] On the other hand, the churches and ecclesial realities that are growing are precisely those that are making highly demanding and countercultural moral proposals: conservative evangelical churches, Pentecostal communities, and the Catholic Church.[48] Why should we as Catholics take our lead from churches and ecclesial realities that are quite objectively declining in attendance, membership, and social influence, some being at the verge of extinction?[49] It is just and right to love and respect our separated brothers and sisters. But this does not mean we should imitate their mistakes, but rather learn from them.

The Church's teaching on sexuality, marriage, and family, as she has consistently taught it along the centuries, is not an obstacle to evangelization. Rather, by promoting the family, this teaching is preparing the soil for people's reception of the Gospel message. As Pope Francis puts it,

The "Good News" of the family is a very important part of evangelization, which Christians can communicate to all, by the witness of their lives; and already they are doing

[47] Mary Eberstadt, *How the West Really Lost God: A New Theory of Secularization* (West Conshohocken, Pa,: Templeton Press, 2013), p. 140.

[48] Ibid., p. 153.

[49] Cf. ibid., 153: "In sum, the churches that did most to loosen up the traditional moral code of Christianity are the same churches that have ended up suffering most for that effort—demographically, financially, morale-wise, and otherwise. Some are on the brink of actual extinction."

so, this is evident in secularized societies: truly Christian families are known by their fidelity, their patience, their openness to life, and by their respect for the elderly ... the secret to this is the presence of Jesus in the family.[50]

Eberstadt notes how statistical data for the Western world clearly suggests a correlation between religiosity and family. While for a long time the dominant view among sociologists was that people become more family focused when they are more religious (more God equals more family), Eberstadt provides substantial statistical evidence that suggests that it is more plausible to think of the influence going the other way, in most cases. According to her, what she calls "the family factor" has a highly relevant impact on people's or a culture's religiosity.[51] Her main thesis, then, can be summarized as the following: more family equals more God; less family equals less God.

If we suppose that she has read the sociological data correctly and that family life indeed favors religious practice, while the demise of the family tends to bring with it the abandonment of such practice, it will still be necessary to give possible reasons for this connection. In her own attempts at an explanation, Eberstadt notices the different ways in which the family opens people up to the transcendent. There is, for one, the moment of

[50] "Address of Pope Francis to Participants in the Plenary Assembly of the Pontifical Council for the Family", Friday, October 25, 2013.

[51] Cf. Eberstadt, *How the West Really Lost God*, p. 22: "Family and faith are the invisible double helix of society—two spirals that when linked to one another can effectively reproduce, but whose strength and momentum depend on one another." Cf. also ibid., p. 98: "It is at least as plausible—in fact, given the evidence ahead, it is *more* plausible—to assume the opposite: *that something about having larger or stronger or more connected families is making people more religious, at least some of the time*" (original emphasis).

childbirth, which "is routinely experienced by a great many people as an event transcendental as no other".[52] In birth, a new human life is manifested. The parents know that they are the authors of this life and that yet the effect exceeds the cause. The child is experienced as something greater than what they could have been responsible for by themselves. Second, it is in the family that people start caring about others more than they care about themselves, which also means opening themselves up to the transcendent. Eberstadt writes: "All men and women fear death; but only mothers and fathers can be counted upon to fear another individual's death more than their own, for almost all do."[53] In the family, people learn what it means to have something to live for and to have something to die for.

To look still deeper into the positive relationship between the family and an individual person's or a culture's openness to God, we can turn to Benedict XVI. In a very suggestive argument, he cites Saint Augustine's famous saying: "Well, if you see charity, yes indeed you see the Trinity."[54] If this is true, then the way of love will be the most convincing "proof" for the existence of God and the high road of evangelization. Now the way of love is intimately linked to the Christian family, since "to the extent it succeeds in living love as communion and service as a reciprocal gift open to all, as a journey of permanent conversion supported by the grace of God, [it] reflects the splendour of Christ in the world and the beauty of the

[52] Ibid., p. 156.

[53] Ibid., p. 159.

[54] Saint Augustine, *On the Trinity* 8.8, quoted in "Address of His Holiness Benedict XVI to Participants at the Plenary Assembly of the Pontifical Council for the Family", December 1, 2011.

divine Trinity".[55] Thus, a family that lives in the communion of the reciprocal gift, and in this way reflects the love that is the very being of God, would have to be among the most convincing evidences for God's existence. The family thus becomes "a saved and a saving community".[56] This is why, for Benedict XVI, "marriage"—and, we may add, the family—"is called to be not only an object but a subject of the new evangelization."[57]

* * * * *

Inasmuch as the Church's moral teaching sustains the family, it sustains the Church's cause of evangelization. But there is an even more direct way in which the Church's proclamation of a way of life furthers the spread of the Gospel. We are referring to the simple fact that people are naturally interested in what directly touches their lives. They may or may not agree, but they do listen. If the Church were to stop speaking out on moral issues, or adapt her position to what is presented by the social media as the mainline consensus, she would exclude herself from the most important cultural debate and render herself insignificant. Morals matter, even, and perhaps especially, to people of our own day. People may be ignorant of or opposed to Christian morality, but they are certainly not indifferent to morality as such. Hospitals are instituting bioethics councils and so are national governments. People

[55] Benedict XVI, "Address to the Pontifical Council for the Family".
[56] FC 49.
[57] "Holy Mass for the Opening of the Synod of Bishops and Proclamation of St. John of Avila and of St. Hildegard of Bingen as 'Doctors of the Church': Homily of His Holiness Pope Benedict XVI", October 7, 2012.

go on the streets to demonstrate against the biogenetic manipulation of plants. They boycott fuels produced by crops, perceptive to the fact that this procedure inevitably causes food prices to rise, consigning man to the threat of starvation.

Even in the field of sexuality, our contemporary culture is much less libertarian than one might expect. While among consenting adults "everything goes", people are keenly aware that nothing must be done against or without the other's consent. There are still moral lines, not written in the sand, but written in stone. Perhaps it is no longer the line between making love to one's wife or to a prostitute, but there certainly remains the line between making love to a prostitute who is of age or to one who is underage. The question of justice, of maturity, and of capacity for consent is central here. We are not living in an age of moral indifference, nor are people generally understanding themselves to be celebrating licentiousness. Advocates of abortion promote it as a *right* to personal autonomy and privacy. Spreading the use of condoms and other contraceptives is considered a moral duty to prevent the disaster of overpopulation and the spread of venereal disease. A pope who questions whether the advocacy of condom use is the right manner to stop the HIV-AIDS epidemic in Africa is not charged with being a moral rigorist and spoilsport, but with being *immoral* or criminal.[58] Said positively, all this goes to show that, for our contemporaries, morality matters.

[58] Cf., for instance, "France and Germany Rebuke Pope over Condom and Aids in Africa Comments", *Telegraph*, March 18, 2009, http://www.telegraph.co.uk/news/worldnews/europe/vaticancityandholysee/5013378/France-and-Germany-Rebuke-Pope-over-condom-and-Aids-in-Africa-comments.html.

The world we live in, sincerely or not, frames all its great concerns in moral terms—we do not go to war for greed or power; we do not want oil or soil but seek to make justice prevail. Our causes for war are morally more noble even than the right to self-defense, the one motive that the Church has always acknowledged to be legitimate. We no longer fight our wars in the name of God (that would be unenlightened), but we do so in the name of morality itself, that is, in the name of justice, which we sought and seek to make prevail in countries such as Bosnia, Afghanistan, Iraq, and Libya. What would happen if in this world the Church renounced speaking about morality? The modern world would no longer find in her an interlocutor about the issues closest to its heart. What is just and what is unjust? How does one live one's life well? Thus, when the Church speaks about moral issues, from contraception and artificial procreation to cloning and genetic manipulation, from premarital sex and divorce to abortion and euthanasia, she has an interlocutor in the modern world. The modern world may not agree—it may be scandalized, if not outraged; it may start media campaigns against individuals or the entire Church; it may, as it has recently happened in France, put Christians in jail for no greater crime than wearing a T-shirt that depicts a family made up of a man, a woman, and their kids[59]—but nonetheless, precisely by showing anger, rage, and incomprehension in front of the Christian moral proposal, the modern world shows that it cares and that it is far removed from the one attitude that is more deadly than opposition, that is, indifference.

[59] Cf. "France: Demonstrators Take to Streets to Call for Anti-Equal Marriage Protester's Release", June 25, 2013, http://vaticaninsider.lastampa.it/en /world-news/detail/articolo/francia-france-francia-25958/.

In fact, the greatest cultural revolution of our days is completely wrapped in moral terms. Gender mainstreaming, that is, the attempts at rendering insignificant the existence of sexual difference, is very often phrased in rights language. Such is the case, for instance, in U.S. President Barack Obama's 2013 inaugural address, in which he proclaims with great pathos the government's moral duty to see to the end of all kinds of discrimination:

> We, the people, declare today that the most evident of truths—that all of us are created equal—is the star that guides us still.... It is now our generation's task to carry on what those pioneers began. For our journey is not complete until our wives, our mothers and daughters can earn a living equal to their efforts. Our journey is not complete until our gay brothers and sisters are treated like anyone else under the law—for if we are truly created equal, then surely the love we commit to one another must be equal as well.[60]

For President Obama, as for many of our contemporaries, love is love, whether it is between people of the opposite sex or of the same sex. And while the potentially universal love of neighbor and enemy was something that our Lord Jesus himself has preached, it is also clear from Scripture and the entire Christian tradition that when it comes to a love that includes the use of the sexual organs, some distinction is not only permitted but also called for. If love is love, however, then sexual difference will be completely indifferent, and so will the question of the potential fruitfulness of a sexual union.

---

[60] "Inaugural Address by President Barack Obama" (United States Capitol, January 21, 2013), http://www.whitehouse.gov/the-press-office/2013/01/21 /inaugural-address-president-barack-obama.

Gender theory builds upon the distinction between sex and gender. While sex is a biological given, gender is socially constructed. And indeed, it seems that one can distinguish between the biological fact of being male or female and the individual or social appropriation and expression of this fact. Hence, Jutta Burggraf writes, "The term *gender* can be accepted as a human, and thus free, expression that is based on the sexual biological identity as male or female. It is appropriate for describing the cultural aspects that turn around the construction of the roles of man and woman in the social context."[61] But the theory of gender goes beyond that. It introduces a rupture between biological sex and social gender, taking to their extreme consequences Simone de Beauvoir's famous words: "One is not born, but rather becomes, a woman."[62] It denies any importance to sexual difference for the formation of one's identity, to the extent that, according to Tony Anatrella, "the concept of sexual orientation replaces the idea of sexual identity, presenting homosexuality, for instance, as an alternative to heterosexuality, which in reality it is not."[63] Thus, whether one feels strictly attracted to people of the opposite sex or whether one sees oneself to belong to one of the LGBT (lesbian, gay, bisexual, transgender) categories tends to become more important for defining one's personal identity than whether one is male or female.

[61] Jutta Burggraf, "Genere (*«gender»*)," in Pontificio Consiglio per la Famiglia, ed. *Lexicon: Termini ambigui e discussi su famiglia, vita e questioni etiche* (Bologna: Edizioni Dehoniane, 2003), p. 428; translation our own.

[62] Simone de Beauvoir, *The Second Sex*, trans. H.M. Parshley (London: Vintage Books, 1997), p. 295.

[63] Tony Anatrella, *La teoria del "gender" e l'origine dell'omosessualità: Una sfida culturale* (Milano: San Paolo, 2012), p. 35; translation our own.

In fact, it would seem that the theory of gender can only arise in a society that has lost any sense of connection between sexual activity and procreation. Only in such a context can sexual preference become more important than sexual difference, with its inherent reference to fruitfulness. If people need to be recognized on the basis of their gender identity, and if gender identity is almost completely unrelated to biological sex, then there will be no objective fact that allows educators to treat boys and girls differently. The best thing for them to do will be to ignore sexual differences altogether, so as to allow children to construct their gender identity spontaneously without interference from adults. The result is that there are already places where the well-known fact that women can become pregnant is minimized in sex education, as if pregnancy were just another venereal disease, which by some grave injustice can afflict only females, but which it is the common responsibility of all involved to avoid. Evidently, simply ignoring the fact that sexuality, that is, sexual difference, exists does not simply cause it to disappear. As the feminist writer Camille Paglia points out, ignoring sexual differences can only have detrimental consequences, which is why she admonishes public schools in America to "Put Sex Back in Sex Ed", appealing to them to acknowledge the crucial difference between boys and girls. With a healthy realism she warns that "it is absurd to avoid the harsh reality that boys have less to lose from casual serial sex than do girls, who risk pregnancy and whose future fertility can be compromised by disease."[64]

---

[64] Camille Paglia, "Put the Sex Back in Sex Ed", *Time*, March 13, 2014, http://time.com/23054/camille-paglia-put-the-sex-back-in-sex-ed/.

In the context of a culture influenced by the theory of gender, it is considered brute biologism to make much of the fact that a sexual "union", however achieved, between people of the same sex is inherently sterile, while a sexual union between a man and a woman is potentially fruitful, and if sterile, only accidentally so. That human procreation is of the highest personal significance is simply denied, contrary to the lived experience of most people of essentially all ages. Even today, isn't becoming a mother or father among the most life-changing and most significant events in a person's life? A man who becomes a father and a woman who becomes a mother are no longer the same. The newly instituted relationship with the child profoundly changes the person's identity, and it also changes the relationship between the man and the woman, who have now become more than two lovers: they have become the father and the mother of each other's child. It is precisely through its procreative dimension that human sexuality discloses a vocation to the human person, a call to transcendence, to going beyond oneself. Today's culture runs the risk of losing sight of all this. The theory of gender proclaims that personal identity is essentially self-assigned and has little to do with fruitfulness or interpersonal relations. As we speak, a new generation is being raised that is completely confused and insecure about its identity. Children must feel that they are no longer allowed to be sons and daughters, that they are not called to be husbands and wives, fathers and mothers. It will be very hard for them to find an answer to the basic question of what to live for. The final cause is the cause of all causes, and they may never know about it. What we desire much more than sexual gratification is that our lives be fruitful, that we leave a mark in someone else's life (and what could be a greater mark in someone's life than to have actually generated someone), that we have not lived in vain but gave life to others. What will happen to a generation that has been taught that any such aspiration is brute biologism?

In the face of the challenge posed to the Church by the theory of gender, Cardinal Kasper's words assume a great urgency: "We may not limit the discussion to the situation of the divorced and remarried."[65] At a time of a radical anthropological revolution, we just cannot allow ourselves to spend time on problems that were relevant some forty years ago, arising only in the context of an at least nominally Christian culture in the West. This culture no longer exists. The present culture in the Western world is one in which our contemporaries are attempting to cancel the truth of creation that "male and female he created them" (Gen 1:27). On top of that, the Catholic Church, in her universality, is larger than the West, where this problem is more acutely felt. By placing undue emphasis on the question of the divorced and remarried, we risk imposing a Eurocentric or Western-centered perspective on the Church as a whole, thus ignoring the interests of some particular churches whose concerns are different.[66]

In contrast, the challenges posed by gender theory bears upon the perspective of the Church universal. Its

---

[65] *Gospel of the Family*, p. 33.

[66] The recently published *Instrumentum Laboris* drafted by the Secretariat of the Synod of Bishops in preparation of the Third Extraordinary General Assembly gives substance to this concern: "The responses indicate that in Europe and across America, a very high number of persons are separated, divorced or divorced and remarried; the number is much lower in Africa and Asia" (n. 86), http://vatican.va/roman_curia/synod/documents/rc_synod_doc_20140626_instrumentum-laboris-familia_en.html.

significance for the proclamation of the Gospel must not be underestimated. A Synod discussing the pastoral challenges to the family in the context of evangelization would certainly do well to address this issue because it touches the heart of Christianity. In his address to the participants of the ecclesial diocesan convention of Rome, in the first months of his pontificate, Benedict XVI attended to a fact that is so obvious that it can be easily overlooked: "The mystery of God's love for men and women receives its linguistic form from the vocabulary of marriage and the family."[67] God has revealed himself to us as *Father*; Jesus calls himself the *Son* of God, raising us up to become God's adopted *sons* and *daughters*, which turns the believers into actual—and all individuals into potential—*brothers* and *sisters*. According to the Scriptures, the Church is the *mother* of all believers (see Gal 4:26) and the *bride* of Christ (see Rev 21:9). What meaning could there be to this Gospel proclamation if people were no longer born and raised in the bosom of a family? They would no longer possess the fundamental experiences at the heart of the Christian faith: spousality, paternity, filiation, and fraternity. The faith would simply become unintelligible to them.

Some Western administrations are already taking gender mainstreaming so far as to erase the words "father" and "mother" from documents and official form sheets, replacing these apparently "reprehensible" terms with the more acceptable expressions "parent 1" and "parent 2". The gender ideology is being introduced into Western school curricula, and if the Church stays silent, within twenty

---

[67] "Address of His Holiness Benedict XVI to the Participants in the Ecclesial Diocesan Convention of Rome", June 6, 2005, p. 5.

years or so the Our *Father* may sound offensive to pious, gender-mainstreamed ears, to the point that parents who are teaching it to their children may well lose custody and gain time in jail. Since the *Catechism of the Catholic Church* calls homosexuality an "inclination, which is objectively disordered" (no. 2358), it may sooner or later end up on the index of governments that are morally more sensitive and are strictly upholding each person's right not to be discriminated against. We see that the stakes are high and that the Church has much to do to proclaim and explain the beauty of sexual difference, which, as Luce Irigaray explains, is *the* issue of our present age.[68] The Church needs to show how sexual difference is connected to our vocation to love and to our calling to live lives that are fruitful. Here, groundbreaking work has been done by John Paul II's theology of the body. We also see the need to explain better that distinguishing and differentiating does not mean discriminating against, that calling a tendency disordered does not mean calling the person who has it a bad person, and that at the same time such a tendency does not justify freely chosen acts by which to live it out.

All this may cost us dearly, which is why it is important that those who teach in the name of the Church recover a sense of the beauty and preciousness of the Gospel message. The Church's charitable activity around the globe adds great strength to her testimony. And yet, she cannot

[68] See Luce Irigaray, *An Ethics of Sexual Difference*, trans. Carolyn Burke and Gillian C. Gill (London: Athlone Press, 1993): "Sexual difference is one of the major philosophical issues, if not the issue, of our age. According to Heidegger, each age has one issue to think through, and one only. Sexual difference is probably the issue in our time which could be our 'salvation' if we thought it through" (p. 5).

be just one among many charitable organizations. As a mere agency for social services the Church is replaceable. Nor is it enough to speak about God's love and mercy without indicating how this love and mercy touches and transforms our lives. God's mercy is a healing mercy that makes us walk. It does not just cover our wounds and sins but transforms us from within.

Faced with the present cultural context, it would be a horrible mistake, even remotely, to give the impression that the Church's teachers themselves do not believe in the indissolubility of marriage, marital faithfulness, marital exclusivity, and the possibility of a chaste abstinence, if this is what love requires in specific life situations. Cardinal Kasper is certainly right to remind us that "one must understand the doctrine of the indissolubility of marriage from the inner connection of the mysteries of faith (so says the First Vatican Council; see DH 3016) and within the hierarchy of the truths of faith (so says the Second Vatican Council in UR 11)."[69] Evidently, this is in consonance with what Francis writes in *Evangelii gaudium*. Citing the Second Vatican Council, he refers to the same fact:

> All revealed truths derive from the same divine source and are to be believed with the same faith, yet some of them are more important for giving direct expression to the heart of the Gospel. In this basic core, what shines forth is the beauty of the saving love of God made manifest in Jesus Christ who died and rose from the dead. In this sense, the Second Vatican Council explained, "in Catholic doctrine there exists an order or a 'hierarchy' of truths, since they vary in their relation to the foundation of the Christian faith." This holds true as much for the dogmas

[69] *Gospel of the Family*, p. 44.

of faith as for the whole corpus of the Church's teaching, including her moral teaching.[70]

If, as the Pope points out, what determines a given doctrine's place in the hierarchy of truths is its more or less immediate relation to the basic core (namely, "the beauty of the saving love of God made manifest in Jesus Christ who died and rose from the dead"), then the teaching on the indissolubility of marriage would certainly have to be allocated at a rather high level in this hierarchy, given that the author of Ephesians refers the relationship between husband and wife to the relationship between Christ and his Church (see Eph 5:32), enabling John Paul II to say that marital infidelity comports breaking "the sign of the covenant and of fidelity to Christ".[71] In other words, if marriage is a real and effective sign of God's covenantal faithfulness, how could the Church's teaching on the indissolubility of marriage and on marital exclusivity not have a rather high standing in the hierarchy of the truths of faith? Not only does God speak to us about marriage, but marriage also speaks to us about God, to the extent that, as Benedict XVI points out, "corresponding to the image of a monotheistic God is monogamous marriage."[72]

1.4. Responsibility, Fear, and Hope as the Synod Approaches

Speaking about the questions connected to the pastoral care of the divorced and remarried, Cardinal Kasper points

[70] *EG* 36.
[71] *FC* 84.
[72] *DCE* 11.

out how "in this matter, there are great expectations in the Church." He acknowledges that "beyond a doubt, we cannot fulfill all expectations", but he admonishes us that "it would cause a terrible disappointment if we would only repeat the answers that supposedly have always been given."[73] Here we must ask, of course, whether this is an appropriate argument. It would seem that if we feel obliged to the truth, as we should, the question of what people expect to hear from us must not influence us in the least. The Cardinal continues, pointing out that "as witnesses of hope, we may not allow ourselves to be led by a hermeneutic of fear."[74] Yet at this point we may wonder whether fear is always something negative. It seems that some things are very reasonably to be feared. Thus, Hans Jonas, in his paramount book *The Imperative of Responsibility*, constructs much of his argument about human responsibility in the age of technology precisely on this: a "heuristics of fear",[75] which for him is not at all the same as timidity or a fear *of* something, but rather a fear *for* something. Of course, we are speaking here of a different context than the one Jonas addresses. He treats of a fear and a responsibility *for* planet earth and *for* humanity, imposing on us a responsibility that is *before* ourselves and *before* future generations. The present argument regards a responsibility of the pastors and teachers of the Church *for* the Gospel and *for* the faithful entrusted to them. It is a responsibility *for* a heritage that is not their own, a responsibility they have before God himself. Whoever feels responsible for something will also

---

[73] *Gospel of the Family*, p. 47.

[74] Ibid.

[75] Hans Jonas, *The Imperative of Responsibility: In Search of an Ethics for the Technological Age* (Chicago: University of Chicago Press, 1984), pp. 26–27.

fear for what he is responsible for. Is it thus really so unreasonable to apply a heuristics of fear to the present context? At some moments a healthy fear should indeed guide us: a fear that we might water down and betray the Gospel; a fear of not telling people the truth of the Gospel or of causing confusion among them regarding its content; a fear of reducing the number of the sacraments from seven to six, if not in words ("doctrine"), then in deeds ("pastoral practice").

But of course we agree with the Cardinal that "some courage and above all biblical candor (*parrhesia*) are necessary."[76] Yet, could this really be the courage to tolerate and ultimately condone extramarital sexual activity? This, again, is what Cardinal Kasper's suggestion amounts to. If indeed he firmly upholds, as he does, that a consummated sacramental marriage is indissoluble, and at the same time proposes to admit to Communion—at least some of—the divorced and remarried who are not professing any intention to abstain from sexual relations, then, by so condoning their objective state of life, he necessarily advocates that the Church legitimize "an extramarital exercise of human sexuality".[77] Is the courage we need really the courage to give up the Church's teaching of two millennia that sex is for conjugal love alone? Would it not rather be the courage to contradict a pansexualistic culture? Would it not be the candor to announce the gospel of the family against all opposition, a gospel that contains as one of its central elements the indissolubility and unity of marriage as an effective sign of God's covenantal faithfulness? Would it not be the hope that the "forever" is really possible, that

---

[76] *Gospel of the Family*, p. 47.
[77] Cf. Caffarra, "Da Bologna con amore" [*From Bologna with Love*].

God gives us his strength and grace to be able to accomplish what we have always desired in the deepest recesses of our hearts?

Toward the end of his booklet, the Cardinal writes, "If we don't want that, then we should not hold a synod on this topic, because then the situation would be worse afterwards than before."[78] The question is what he means by "this topic". The immediate context suggests that what he refers to is the issue of admitting to Communion the faithful who are divorced and civilly remarried and who do not wish to follow the practice proposed by *Familiaris consortio* and *Sacramentum caritatis*. The larger context would seem to contradict this interpretation. Earlier in his presentation he, quite justly, points out that one may not reduce the problem of the divorced and remarried "to the question of admission to communion",[79] and, a little later on, in a passage already cited, he clearly affirms that "we may not limit the discussion [about the gospel of the family, and thus presumably about the topic of the Synod] to the situation of the divorced and remarried or to many other difficult pastoral situations that have not been mentioned in this context." Rather, we should "begin positively, discovering and proclaiming again the gospel of the family in its total beauty".[80] To these words nothing needs to be added and nothing needs to be detracted.

[78] *Gospel of the Family*, p. 47.
[79] Ibid., p. 25.
[80] Ibid., p. 33.

2

The Truth of Sacramental Marriage: Where Mercy and Faithfulness Meet

The expression that serves as the guiding light for our book, "mercy and faithfulness",[1] occurs in the Wisdom literature as a true, proper definition of God: "Mercy and faithfulness will meet" (Ps 85:10). Both terms make a significant allusion to the *covenant*, to which they refer as the foundation of a wondrous union of the two.[2] Therefore it

---

[1] Cf. *Gospel of the Family*, p. 26: "Mercy and fidelity belong together".

[2] As explained by Cardinal Kasper, in *Mercy: The Essence of the Gospel and the Key to Christian Life*, trans. William Madges (New York/Mahwah, N.J.: Paulist Press, 2014), p. 49: "God descends to Moses in a cloud, as a sign of his mysterious presence, and calls out to him: 'The LORD, the LORD, a God merciful [*rachum*] and gracious [*henun*], slow to anger, and abounding in steadfast love [*hesed*] and faithfulness [*emet*]' (Exod 34:6). In this third revelation of his name, mercy is not only an expression of God's sovereignty and freedom; it is also an expression of his fidelity.... It became, so to speak, the credo of the Old Testament." This is a good description of its importance, although it lacks a definition of its connection with the covenant that, in contrast, is a fundamental point, as expressed in John Paul II, Encyclical Letter *Dives in misericordia*, November 30, 1980, no. 4, n. 52: "First there is the term *hesed*, which indicates a profound attitude of 'goodness.' When this is established between two individuals, they do not just wish each other well; they are also faithful to each other by virtue of an interior commitment, and therefore also by virtue of a *faithfulness to themselves*. Since *hesed* also means 'grace' or 'love,' this occurs precisely on the basis of this *fidelity*.... When in the Old Testament the word *hesed* is used of the Lord, this always occurs in connection with the covenant that God established with Israel" (emphasis added).

63

is not something derived from the idea of God as Creator, but rather from God's self-manifestation in his historical revelation, in his way of making himself present within our lives and in a manner in which he can be recognized. Within this context of the covenant, the two terms are correlated with the divine will for man and have to do with the latter's response, without which the covenant is impossible.

2.1. A Place in Which God Is Revealed

As far as their etymology is concerned, the terms "mercy" and "faithfulness" are very different, which means that their encounter is not merely a Semitic repetition but is revelatory of the mystery of God. Mercy (*hesed*) is more affective; it is connected with the idea of abiding in the covenant as a *bond* that generates interiorly the ability to overcome the obstacles opposed to it;[3] the second term, "faithfulness" (*'emet*), is more cognitive, in the context of experiential knowledge, and refers to the firmness characteristic of the Word of God that grants a unique certitude to man. Both terms therefore share in a temporal continuity that is of divine origin. The invocation "his mercy endures forever" (*kî leʿôlām hasdô*), which in one psalm becomes a litany (see Ps 136), is therefore a supplication of someone who knows that by his prayer he obtains a blessing from heaven.

---

[3] Cardinal Kasper defines it as follows in *Mercy*, p. 43: "The most important expression for understanding mercy is *hesed*, which means unmerited loving kindness, friendliness, favor and also divine grace and mercy. *Hesed*, therefore, goes beyond mere emotion and grief at human deprivation; it means God's free and gracious turning toward the human person with care."

In order to understand more fully the content of our experience, we need to consider that these qualities appear as a divine response to human weakness, through which man takes part in a characteristic of God's action. In biblical terminology, they are attributed almost exclusively to God, but always with respect to their effect on needy mankind.

In particular, faithfulness (*'emet*) is connected with faith; the believer's assent to this divine faithfulness is derived from it: the yes of the *amén* (from the root *'āman*).[4]

The firmness implied in this "yes" is superior to specifically human firmness; by means of faith, man indeed becomes a witness to the faithfulness (*'emet*) of God. Its connection with mercy is therefore a way of showing that the specific object of Christian faith is love, and this confers on it a set of specific characteristics that are far removed from mere compassion.

The summit of this union is found in a Person, Christ, the One who is "full of grace and truth" (Jn 1:14). His manifest fullness is contrasted to the preceding moment at the heart of the plan of salvation: "For the law was given through Moses; grace and truth came through Jesus Christ" (Jn 1:17). In both cases we find before us an interesting interpretation: in this case *hesed* is translated by *cháris* (grace), while *'emet* is rendered by *alétheia* (truth).[5] In Saint

---

[4] See Kasper, *Mercy*, pp. 54–55: "This sovereign freedom is no arbitrary freedom. It also is not the expression of a spontaneous, so to speak, instinctive and solicitous attention to the misery of his people. Rather, it is the expression of his fidelity (*emet*).... In the New Testament, *aman* is translated as, πιστεύειν that is, to believe."

[5] See D. Muñoz León, *Proclamación del Evangelio de S. Juan* (Madrid: Edice, 1988), p. 195: "The expression 'grace and truth' in this case corresponds to the Hebrew חסד ואמת, *hesed we'emet* of the psalms, which sing the goodness and the faithfulness, the mercy and the fidelity of God."

John's theology this is a way of highlighting the *personal* significance that they acquire in Christ as revelation of the Father.[6] In him, the union between God's mercy (his salvific action of praise) and his faithfulness as man is a union in the *flesh* that recapitulates all of history in its utmost concreteness.

As Kasper correctly recalls, in the biblical tradition mercy and truth are inseparable,[7] and this profound union ought to shed light on the action of the Church. Thus Saint Paul calls on us to do "the truth in love" (Eph 4:15).[8] This means being aware of a truth of love that possesses its own logic and should guide the life of the Church as well as that of society, as Pope Benedict XVI very profoundly taught us in *Caritas in veritate*, where he attributes to love a social value of great originality.[9] In order for there to be

---

[6] See Ignace De la Potterie, *La vérité dans saint Jean*, I, *Le Christ et la vérité: L'Esprit et la vérité* (Rome: Biblical Institute Press, 1977).

[7] See *Gospel of the Family*, p. 44: "Mercy is bound to the truth, but conversely the truth is also bound to mercy." This is how the Cardinal had entitled the article published in *L'Osservatore Romano* (March 11, 2014), which was then included in the booklet as "Concluding Comment on the Discussion" (pp. 43–47).

[8] Cited in *Gospel of the Family*, p. 44. The meaning of this might be the following: "Theologically, the point is to do the truth in love (Eph 4:15), that is, to do what is right, guided by love" (*Mercy*, p. 180).

[9] See Benedict XVI, Encyclical Letter *Caritas in veritate*, June 29, 2009, no. 2:

I am aware of the ways in which charity has been and continues to be misconstrued.... Hence the need to link charity with truth not only in the sequence, pointed out by Saint Paul, of *veritas in caritate* (Eph 4:15), but also in the inverse and complementary sequence of *caritas in veritate*. Truth needs to be sought, found and expressed within the "economy" of charity, but charity in its turn needs to be understood, confirmed and practised in the light of truth. In this way, not only do we do a service to charity enlightened by truth, but we also help give credibility to truth, demonstrating its persuasive and authenticating power in the practical setting of social living. This is a matter of no small account

an effective union, it must be brought about in the life of a people that lives out and witnesses to mercy;[10] therefore, the dimension in question is not private but universal and evangelizing. This is what ought to animate the pastoral ministry of the Church.

2.2. Their Light in the History of a Nuptial Love

This "meeting place" of mercy and faithfulness requires a historical action of God within a people if it is to be significant in the midst of human beings. This is why it is incorporated into the central and foundational event of the biblical tradition: the covenant.

The covenant is established as the foundation of the *spousal analogy* of God with his people—a pivotal consideration in which the depths of God's love are revealed. God unites himself to Israel as a bridegroom to his bride. Of all things, the polygamous environment in which Israel lives helps us to understand the genuine content of this divine self-revelation.[11] A fundamental moment of this revelation is the Song of Songs, which collects and unifies the Wisdom literature that illumines the human experience of love in terms of the light of the divine vision, as well

---

today, in a social and cultural context which relativizes truth, often paying little heed to it and showing increasing reluctance to acknowledge its existence.

This dimension is studied in Juan José Pérez-Soba and M. Magdič, eds., *L'amore principio di vita sociale: "Caritas aedificat" (1 Cor 8,1)* (Siena: Cantagalli, 2011).

[10] This topic is discussed in Kasper, *Mercy*, pp. 181–205.

[11] See Luis Alonso Schökel, *Símbolos matrimoniales en la Biblia* (Estella: Verbo Divino, 1997).

as the *prophetic* literature, which testifies to God's loving presence in the midst of his people in concrete historical reality. The love experienced by the believer is profoundly new, born of an unconditional commitment that goes far beyond any merely human measure.[12]

Benedict XVI showed this when he declared:

> Corresponding to the image of a monotheistic God is monogamous marriage. Marriage based on exclusive and definitive love becomes the icon of the relationship between God and his people and vice versa. God's way of loving becomes the measure of human love. This close connection between *eros* and marriage in the Bible has practically no equivalent in extra-biblical literature.[13]

This biblical innovation displayed an astonishing *exclusivity*. In it we can recognize the space where the personal value of God is revealed, who grants us a new way to love: the way he loves us. This figures as "primordial love"[14] in the Encyclical *Lumen fidei*, by Pope Francis; it is essential in understanding how this first divine gift unites all persons with respect to the meaning of their lives in the Love that created them.

[12] The pivotal truth of the revelation in the Song of Songs is summarized thus by G. Ravasi in *Il Cantico dei cantici* (Bologna: Edizioni Dehoniane, 1992), p. 670: "In the wake of prophetic theology, Israel, converted and cleansed of her sin, receives from God the promise of an unbreakable, eternal covenant. Divine love is transcendent and victorious over death, evil, chaos, nothingness; it is an inextinguishable flame."

[13] *DCE* 11. This is the conclusion of the biblical survey conducted in nos. 9–10.

[14] See *LF* 51: "Faith is born of an encounter with God's primordial love, wherein the meaning and goodness of our life become evident; our life is illumined to the extent that it enters into the space opened by that love, to the extent that it becomes, in other words, a path and praxis leading to the fullness of love."

Naturally, this personal loving relationship with God structures the history of salvation; herein we find the principal reasons for our faith. This confirms for us the *central* position of marriage in the hierarchy of Christian truths[15] and, therefore, of its essential characteristics, the initial foundation of which is rooted in divine mercy.

Thus two realities emerge that structure the life of the people of Israel and will be essential for the Church. The first is the truth of the *promise* that is constitutive of marriage and, at the same time, foundational for the covenant. The very history of Israel finds in this promise the source of the *revelation* of God, especially when, with the experience of the exile, its content ceases to be the land, the temple, and the king, which in fact no longer exist, and a *New Covenant* is promised in the heart of a people that can, by divine mercy, return to being faithful. The content of the promise, by way of conversion, thus becomes an intimate and universal truth.[16]

The other truth is the fact that the foundation of the covenant is inseparably linked to the analogy between adultery and idolatry, as a way of indicating the strength of God's presence in marriage. The parallelism has nothing to do with the mere transgression of a law, but it concerns the *heart* of man. As is natural, given the greater importance that the people of Israel assigned to idolatrous infidelity, the purpose of the similitude contained in revelation is not to show the obvious malice of idolatry, but rather to situate it in a *new context* that is no longer simply legal but also affective, since it thus allows us to understand God's

[15] For a statement of this, see *EG* 36.
[16] See Carlos Granados García, *La nueva alianza como recreación: estudio exegético de Ez 36, 16–38* (Rome: Analecta Biblica, 2010).

surprising reaction. This is no longer a simple cultic question whereby adoration must be addressed to one God numerically (which could be called *henotheism*); now, instead, we enter into the context of the loving communication, full of affective reminiscences, of a God who gives himself. This is how *exclusivity* must be understood in the presence of a God who is jealous of his people.[17] This is a question of the heart and the emotions, rather than of external law. We see that God's life involves intimacy and affections—he wants an *exclusive* covenant with his people. Marriage, as a bond between a man and a woman, enters into the mystery of a plan of God, who makes himself present in the nuptial covenant of human love and manifests himself in it.

Within this setting arrives the revelation of the *divine mercy*, the purpose of which is to preserve the bond of the covenant with God as something definitive and, consequently, indissoluble. Therefore it must overcome the chief trial: the fragility of man, who seems unequal to the demands of a union of this type. We need to be assured that this promised covenant can overcome what seems in and of itself to be a definitive rupture: the sin of the people.

2.3. Sin and Hardness of Heart

As is well-known, the external signs of the covenant change with the loss of Israel's political independence. *Circumcision* is resumed as a reference point that is linked to the succession of generations as a bond with the covenant

[17] See Antonio Sicari, *Matrimonio e verginità nella rivelazione: L'uomo di fronte alla "Gelosia di Dio"* (Milan: Jaca Book, 1978).

of the patriarchs. These means establish the permanence of a kind of faithfulness as a filial promise that is received along with the transmission of life. It is the sign of a divine choice that precedes us and principally structures our freedom. Now, with respect to the New Covenant, the Deuteronomic metaphor is retrieved with a "circumcision of the heart"[18] that can only be the work of the divine action and requires a conversion of the people.

The same revelation of God's spousal love has a direct bearing on the sin of infidelity, with the clear intention of defeating it *definitively*. The force of the image, therefore, goes beyond the metaphor, so as to insist on the divine *newness* that is revealed, which consists in the forgiveness of infidelity: a divine grace that transforms the heart to make it return to being faithful to a covenant that sin has not broken in its most profound reality, since it persists in the merciful heart of God.[19] This by no means implies tolerating infidelity, considering it unimportant or a lesser

---

[18] This was proclaimed already in Deuteronomy 10:16: "Circumcise therefore the foreskin of your heart, and be no longer stubborn", but especially in Deuteronomy 30:4, 6: "If your outcasts are in the uttermost parts of heaven, from there the LORD your God will gather you, and from there he will fetch you.... And the LORD your God will circumcise your heart and the heart of your offspring, so that you will love the LORD your God with all your heart and with all your soul, that you may live." The root of this action is in Deuteronomy 30:3: "[T]he LORD your God will restore your fortunes, and have compassion upon you."

[19] Hence the analogy of a divine *sorrow* over man's sin; see John Paul II, Encyclical Letter *Dominum et vivificantem*, May 18, 1986, no. 39: "Revealing the pain, unimaginable and inexpressible, on account of sin, the Book of Genesis in its anthropomorphic vision seems to glimpse in the 'depths of God' and in a certain sense in the very heart of the ineffable Trinity. The Church, taking her inspiration from Revelation, believes and professes that sin is an offense against God." This idea is nicely developed in Kasper, *Mercy*, pp. 117–21.

evil that is, in the final analysis, acceptable. Quite the contrary: this sin that violates fidelity is presented by way of
a comparison with an act of adultery, since in both cases a
covenant is broken and for man this is the worst evil of
all. God desires the conversion of sinful man that brings
him back to the life of the covenant as the fruit of mercy.
The aim is to overcome infidelity with reconciliation, by
creating a new *faithful* union so as to return to the original
union with a greater love.[20]

In this sense, the divine response to man's sin is the offer
of the *forgiveness* that is born of mercy as its mature fruit.
True knowledge of the internal dynamic of forgiveness
enables us to understand better the meaning of mercy:

> The response springs from the divine depths. Confronted
> with man's sin, God responds with *per-dono* [pardon]. This
> word is composed etymologically of the prefix *per-* indi-
> cating thoroughness or perfection: *per-dono* is the *perfect
> gift*; it means "to go back to giving oneself". Thus pardon
> goes to the root of the sin, the rejection of the gift; pun-
> ishment misses that mark, because it can only inhibit the
> external action. Sin consists not only of disrupting an order
> or breaking some commandments, but in the rejection
> of God's own "self-gift", and it can be conquered only
> through a new love that unites the sinner with God.[21]

The change that God asks for is a change that gives real
substance to the call to conversion. In biblical language,
conversion refers in this context to a "return to the

[20] See Alonso Schökel, *Simbolos matrimoniales en la Biblia*, pp. 153–78. In this
section entitled "Infidelidad y reconciliación" (Infidelity and Reconciliation),
he assigns great importance to the achievement of this reconciliation.

[21] Livio Melina, José Noriega, and Juan José Pérez-Soba, *Camminare nella
luce dell'amore: I fondamenti della morale cristiana* (Siena: Cantagalli, 2010), p. 445.

Covenant", without which it makes no sense.[22] Moreover, thanks to the experience of exile, which made Israel
understand quite clearly that the action of its God reaches
every place, mercy attains a universal value with respect to
a divine plan that is present in creation.

The uncircumcised heart, which does not benefit from
this action of conversion but becomes self-enclosed, far
from the Lord, is what is called in Greek "hardness of
heart", *sklerokardía*.[23] It is a heart that refuses interiorly to
live according to the covenant, although it scrupulously observes the precepts of the Law. The New Covenant strikes
man in the depths of his soul, or in his "heart", which must
pass from infidelity to fidelity. The permanence of this
new union between God and man, which is indissoluble in
Christ, becomes a permanent offer: "if we are faithless, he
remains faithful—for he cannot deny himself" (2 Tim 2:13).

In conquering sin, the binomial mercy-fidelity, enriched
by the binomial grace-truth, acquires a different meaning.
The Latin term *misericordia*, unlike the Hebrew *hesed* (mercy),
highlights the aspect of overcoming human misery,[24] in a

---

[22] See Jan Alberto Soggin, "שוב, *šūb*. Volver", in Ernst Jenni and Claus Wes-
termann, *Diccionario teológico manual del Antiguo Testamento* (Madrid: Ediciones
Cristiandad, 1983), 2:1115: "This must not be understood as though everything
had to return to the former state; it means rather that this 'return' is only the
point of departure for a fully new beginning."

[23] See Friedrich Baumgärtel and Johannes Behm, "*Kardia*", in Gerhard Kittel
and Gerhard W. Friedrich, eds., *Theological Dictionary of the New Testament*,
trans. Geoffrey W. Bromiley, 10 vols. (Grand Rapids, Mich.: Eerdmans, 1965),
III: 605-14.

[24] According to the expression of Saint Augustine, in *De moribus Ecclesiae cath-
olicae* 27.53 (PL 32:1333): "miserum cor faciat condolentis alieno malo" ([mercy]
makes unhappy the heart of someone who has compassion on another's suffering); also, Saint Thomas Aquinas, in *ST* II–II, q. 30, a. 1, states: "dicitur
enim misericordia ex eo quod aliquis habet miserum cor super miseria alterius."
(Mercy takes its name *misericordia* from denoting a man's compassionate heart
for another's unhappiness.)

sense that tends to emphasize the overcoming of sin and death. First of all, it is clear that God's faithfulness with regard to his covenant is the authentic root of *misericordia* (mercy). God's merciful action aims to make man faithful and, once fidelity is recovered (thanks to God's gift), it makes him capable of living in accordance with the demands of his truth.

In this case, the Christological dimension of the union between mercy and faithfulness becomes decisive: Christ as man is the one who realizes the full truth of man in his total fidelity to the Father's will and thus becomes the source of pardon and forgiveness for all of mankind. We therefore recognize in him the utmost expression of his mercy through the union that he establishes between creation and redemption, a greater *truth* that only mercy reveals.

Christ's merciful heart is the definitive defeat of the *sklerokardía* (hardness of heart) caused by sin. His merciful actions, which show above all the most profound affection of his heart, are liberating for the sinner. This is the fulfillment of the prophecy of Hosea about a new union with God: "I desire mercy and not sacrifice" (Hos 6:6), which Christ adopts as a manifesto of his mission.[25] Mercy is the key for living the definitive truth of man's being, which combines his value as a creature with a consideration of his sinful condition and overcomes the latter by the power of redemptive grace.

This is the terminology that Jesus Christ would use to discuss the question about divorce.[26] This is why Jesus

---

[25] Cf. Mt 9:13; 12:7. This has a Christological meaning; see Joachim Gnilka, *Il Vangelo di Matteo*, "Commentario Teologico del Nuovo Testamento, I/1" (Bari: Paideia, 1990), p. 488: "His [Christ's] behavior however becomes the model. His disciples must follow it."

[26] See Luis Sánchez Navarro, *Retorno al principio: La revelación del amor en la Sagrada Escritura* (Burgos: Monte Carmelo, 2010), p. 80: "In Matthew, hardness of heart appears only in relation with divorce; thus it is presented as a special manifestation of the rebellious spirit that is opposed to the Covenant."

will be the one to introduce his maxim into this scenario: "What therefore God has joined together, let no man put asunder" (Mt 19:6). The evangelist puts this passage immediately after the section with the parables about divine mercy (see Mt 18:10–14, 21–35), which are included in the so-called ecclesiastical discourse. He offers us here an image of the community of believers (*ekklesía*) as a society structured by fraternal correction (see Mt 18:15–20) and the practice of mercy. Within this ecclesial setting of the Church's merciful mission, the real value of Christian marriage must be understood as the testimony of a new love within mankind, which reestablishes God's true design that had been obscured by sin.

The explicit mention of a divine gift (see Mt 19:11) that enables man to accept this requirement points out two truths: in the first place, the *real and concrete* meaning of the requirement, which is neither metaphorical nor spiritual, nor merely exemplary, but which involves the personal life of all human beings. In the second place, it requires us to understand the reception of a gift that is not arbitrary but rather is offered as part of the vocation to marriage. In this case, the obligatory parallel is once again baptism as a gift of faith. Since "not all have faith" (2 Thess 3:2), the concrete actualization of its reception is never exclusionary but tends to have universal import. It is absurd to propose an exception to one of these two demands, which are based on a divine intention. Both corroborate the historical truth of the New Covenant lived out under the banner of matrimony, within the context of the revelation of God's salvific love which, being merciful, is universal.[27]

---

[27] See Kasper, *Mercy*, p. 111: "Mercy courts every human being to the very end."

Consequently, the maxim "[w]hat therefore God has joined together, let no man put asunder" (Mt 19:6) acquires, in Christ's words, the definitive meaning that the Church recognizes as a sacrament of the New Covenant, a real sign of this definitive bond of God with mankind. By means of the gift that God offers to Christian spouses, the indissoluble union of marriage is the "place" in which God unites the merciful love that the sacrament grants with the gift of faithfulness offered by grace to man so that he might be capable of living it out in keeping with the New Law.[28] Indissolubility is not in the first place a juridical requirement, but rather it is a direct expression of the merciful love of the Father.

2.4. Mercy and Justice

"Mercy and faithfulness will meet; righteousness and peace will kiss each other" (Ps 85:11). In the union of the two halves of this psalm verse, the term placed in parallel with mercy is *justice*. Mercy as a virtue is not foreign to justice. In this sense, as Kasper correctly states, we cannot leave room for an unjust mercy, since that would be a profound falsification of divine revelation. This happens when a good that involves human dignity is impaired.[29]

---

[28] As defined by Saint Thomas Aquinas, in *ST* I–II, q. 106, a. 1: "est gratia Spiritus Sancti, quae datur per fidem Christi." ([This] is the grace of the Holy Ghost, which is given through faith in Christ.) Cited in Latin by Kasper in *Gospel of the Family*, p. 4, where he refers also to *EG* 37, which in turn cites *ST* I–II, q. 108, a. 1: "principalitas legis novae est gratia spiritus sancti, quae manifestatur in fide per dilectionem operante." (The New Law consists chiefly in the grace of the Holy Ghost, which is shown forth by faith that worketh through love); the last phrase is an implicit citation of Galatians 5:6.

[29] See Kasper, *Mercy*, p. 147: "A further grave misunderstanding of mercy occurs if, in the name of mercy, we think we may ignore God's commandment

In this case, the justice that we are speaking about is not an agreement between human beings, but rather a union with God. We are dealing with something much greater than a merely human order, and therefore it cannot be understood here as mere legal justice. It is necessary to analyze its foundation. On this point, in his address, Kasper follows what he had previously set forth in his book *Mercy*, wherein he takes pride in citing Saint Thomas Aquinas as his source. Let us therefore, in turn, take the saintly Doctor as the guide of our brief examination.

In order to explain this passage, Aquinas specifically cites Psalm 85, which, however, in the Vulgate version that he used says: "misericordia et veritas obviaverunt sibi" (mercy and *truth* have met).[30] This is why, in the order in which he arranges his questions, he introduces truth as the link that unites mercy and justice,[31] in order to point out that one can never work *against* justice but one can act *beyond* it, and this is precisely the space opened up by divine mercy. An unjust action, therefore, is never merciful. What differentiates mercy from mere compassion is the fact that the aim of mercy is to "dispel the misery of another";[32] in other words, mercy is *active* against the evil that the other is enduring. A false consolation that leads someone to say that it is a lesser evil is not mercy if the person enduring it is not freed from it.

---

of justice.... One cannot advise or provide assistance for an abortion out of a phony sense of mercy.... Just as little can one, out of pity for an incurably sick person, offer active assistance in committing suicide."

[30] *ST* I, q. 21, a. 2, sed contra (in the Vulgate it is Psalm 84).

[31] The structure of q. 21 of the *Prima pars* is the following: a. 1, Justice; a. 2, Truth; a. 3, Mercy; a. 4, Relation between mercy and justice.

[32] *ST* I, q. 21, a. 3: "repellere miseriam alterius"; cf. ibid.: "omnem defectum expellunt" (expel every defect); *ST* II–II, q. 30, a. 4: "defectus aliorum sublevet" (supplies the defects of his neighbors).

Kasper very pertinently points out the clear supremacy, proposed by the Angelic Doctor, of mercy as opposed to justice as a divine attribute, in contrast to a tradition of justice alone, as represented by the heritage of Anselm.[33] Nevertheless, he insufficiently develops the fundamental reason for this, that is, the internal *order* of the action, inasmuch as it springs from *love*. This is why the most forceful statement about mercy made by our saint, "The work of divine justice always presupposes the work of mercy and is founded thereupon",[34] is nothing but a parallel of the following statement: "Therefore it is evident that every agent, whatever it be, does every action from love of some kind."[35] Rather than a metaphysics of mercy, what we find in Saint Thomas' writings is a highly developed metaphysics of love,[36] as is demonstrated very clearly from his own words: "God takes pity on us [i.e.,

---

[33] See Kasper, *Mercy*, p. 100: "For this reason, Thomas asserts the original biblical motif of the priority of mercy over against modes of thinking that are one-sidedly oriented to punitive justice."

[34] *ST* I, q. 21, a. 4: "Opus autem divinae iustitiae semper praesupponit opus misericordiae, et in eo fundatur."

[35] *ST* I–II, q. 28, a. 6: "Unde manifestum est quod omne agens, quodcumque sit, agit quamcumque actionem ex aliquo amore."

[36] In fact, practically the only reference that Kasper gives for this metaphysics of mercy is Yves Congar, "La miséricorde, attribut souverain de Dieu", *La vie spirituelle* 482 (April 1962): 380–95. In reality, this very brief and simple article speaks very little about this metaphysical level, and the one time that it does so (p. 390) it is with the citations from Saint Thomas that are the basis of the metaphysics of love (cf. *ST* I, q. 21, a. 3 and 4; Saint Thomas Aquinas, *In Eph.*, c. 2, lect. 2; Saint Thomas Aquinas, *Summa contra gentiles*, lib. 3, c. 150; *ST* I, q. 20, a. 2; of these citations the last two do not even mention mercy; the citation from the *Commentary on the Letter to the Ephesians* can be considered as the one that unites the first two to the others). For references to many Thomistic studies about this metaphysics of love, we take the liberty of recommending Juan José Pérez-Soba, *Amore: introduzione a un mistero* (Siena: Cantagalli, 2012), 46–52.

shows us mercy] through love alone, in as much as He loves us as belonging to Him."[37] Mercy should be understood as "the root of God's love",[38] because it manifests itself in such a way as to consist in an affective principle; in other words, it is the union of love between the love and the beloved, which is the principle of every action.[39] Indeed, in any human action whatsoever, mercy as a virtue is governed by charity,[40] which attributes to it the correct view; above all, it acts in such a way as to turn always toward *union with God*, or in other words, toward living out the covenant with him.

This mention of the dynamic of love as the foundation of mercy is not accidental, but rather introduces us to a dynamism made up of *two objects*: the beloved and the good that it communicates to him, which are both included

---

[37] *ST* II–II, q. 30, a. 2, ad 1: "Deus non miseretur nisi propter amorem, inquantum amat nos tanquam aliquid sui."

[38] See Aquinas, *In Eph.*, c. 2, lect. 2, no. 86: "Amor autem quo Deus amat nos, causat in nobis bonitatem, et ideo misericordia ponitur hic quasi radix amoris divini."

[39] See *ST* I–II, q. 28, a. 6, ad 2: "Unde omnis actio quae procedit ex quacumque passione, procedit etiam ex amore, sicut ex prima causa." (Therefore every act that proceeds from any passion proceeds also from love as from a first cause.) He understands this affect as follows in *ST* I–II, q. 28, a. 2: "Amans vero dicitur esse in amato secundum apprehensionem inquantum amans non est contentus superficiali apprehensione amati, sed nititur singula quae ad amatum pertinent intrinsecus disquirere, et sic ad interiora eius ingreditur." (The lover is said to be in the beloved, according to apprehension, inasmuch as the lover is not satisfied with a superficial apprehension of the beloved, but strives to gain an intimate knowledge of everything pertaining to the beloved, so as to penetrate into his very soul.)

[40] See *ST* II–II, q. 30, a. 4: "Et ideo quantum ad hominem, qui habet Deum superiorem, caritas, per quam Deo unitur, est potior quam misericordia." (Hence, as regards man, who has God above him, charity, which unites him to God, is greater than mercy.) Union with God is the greatest good that can be obtained and communicated to man.

in the truth of the act of loving.[41] This dynamic is essential to an understanding of how mercy is communicated to the sinner. The sinner is loved, but the good that the lover intends to communicate has as its purpose conversion from sin, making sure that the sinner does not remain in sin, since it is an evil for him. Thereby, divine mercy is directly reunited with justice, and thus it has nothing to do with any sort of *tolerance with respect to the sin*; rather it is about seeking the conversion of the sinner, which may take time.

The truth of the *indissoluble marital bond*, which we discussed earlier as a concrete, historical revelation of God's definitive love, therefore fits perfectly into this idea of justice, as a good that must be preserved in a unique way in the New Covenant. Therefore mercy with regard to a person who has been unfaithful to this union does not consist in declaring that the covenant no longer exists, or that it has been destroyed irremediably,[42] but rather consists in affirming that there is a "greater justice" that is possible only thanks to the divine gift that springs from God's pardon. All this notwithstanding, any act of pardon or of mercy can be understood only in terms of the intention to reestablish the lost justice by means of the grace of reconciliation.

[41] See Aquinas, *Summa contra gentiles*, lib. 1, c. 91, no. 763: "aliae operationes animae sint circa unum solum obiectum, solus amor ad duo obiecta ferri videtur. . . . Amor vero aliquid alicui vult, hoc enim amare dicimur cui aliquod bonum volumus." (The other operations of the soul deal with only one object; love alone seems to be directed to two objects. . . . Love, however, wills something for someone, for we are said to love the thing to which we wish some good.) For the dynamic of love, see Juan José Pérez-Soba, *Amor es nombre de persona I, q. 37, a. 1: Estudio sobre la interpersonalidad en el amor en San Tommaso d'Aquino* (Rome: Mursia, 2001).

[42] See also the reflection by F. X. Durrwell in "Indissoluble et destructible mariage", *Revue de Droit Canonique* 36 (1986): 214–42.

Consequently, it is correct to affirm that "mercy is the hermeneutical principle for the interpretation of truth."[43] This therefore is about the "higher righteousness"[44] with a twofold meaning: it is "greater" because it is capable of regenerating the justice that has been violated, by means of an unearned pardon, something that justice alone cannot do; on the other hand, it defends justice so that the transgression against justice does not appear to be an obvious sign of a lack of mercy. To ask mercy to find exceptions to justice would be to set out on the wrong path. Pardon is not an unjust act, but rather goes beyond justice inasmuch as it is not something due, and this is even more true in God's case. The desire of authentic pardon is to return to justice, repairing what the injustice violated. This is required if mercy is to be complete; it restores justice in a higher order, but never goes against justice, for instance, by trying to justify infidelity.

Therefore, divine mercy must be understood as something very different from the mere tolerance of an evil, and never as an implicit acceptance of a sin. It is clear that God tolerates evil, and in particular sin, with a view to a greater good; nevertheless, according to the Angelic Doctor, this always occurs in the specific moral truth of the action, in other words, with reference to the order of justice that can be surpassed yet is still present.[45] Therefore,

---

[43] *Gospel of the Family*, p. 44.

[44] Ibid., p. 29. Further on he speaks about "the higher righteousness" (p. 50), implicitly citing Aquinas (*ST* I, q. 21, a. 3, ad 2), who refers to mercy as "iustitiae plenitudo" (the fullness of justice). First he had cited Kasper, *Mercy*, p. 70: "the greater and higher righteousness of his [Jesus'] heavenly Father".

[45] See *ST* I, q. 21, a. 1: "ita ordo universi, qui apparet tam in rebus naturalibus quam in rebus voluntariis, demonstrat Dei iustitiam." (The order of the universe, which is seen both in effects of nature and in effects of will, shows forth the justice of God.)

in the case of sin, God tolerates the fact that it is committed in view of the future repentance of the sinner whom
he loves. Mercy springs from love for the person in order
to cure him of the sickness of infidelity that afflicts him
and prevents him from living in the covenant with God.
This is something quite different from consenting to the
infidelity without an interior transformation by means of
grace, as though God covered our sins without converting
the heart by cleansing it. This is an important dogmatic
difference between the Catholic concept of justification
and the Lutheran concept.

A kind of mercy that left us in our sinful condition
would not have reached the goal of its dynamism, which
always seeks conversion and purification of heart so that
the penitent can share in the status of beloved son in the
Son, united to the Father in concord. Where there is true
mercy, there is no sin.

> According to Catholic doctrine, no mercy, neither divine
> nor human, entails consent to the evil or tolerance of the
> evil. Mercy is always connected with the moment that
> leads from evil to good. Where there is mercy, evil surren-
> ders. When the evil persists, there is no mercy, but let us
> add: where there is no mercy, the evil continues. Indeed,
> good cannot spring from evil.[46]

"Faithfulness will spring up from the ground, and righteousness will look down from heaven" (Ps 85:11). The
Christian believer who receives the gift of mercy is the

---

[46]Karol Wojtyla, *Mi visión del hombre* [A Spanish anthology of essays on eth-
ics] (Madrid: Palabra, 1997), p. 67, from the essay entitled "On the Problem of
Truth and Mercy". (Citation translated from the Spanish.)

ground that promises fruitfulness through his faithful
response and becomes capable of the divine justice of
union with God; in other words, he is enabled to live
according to his plan. This is the truth of a life that is
generated and grows, not the truth of an objective that
is attained. The dynamic of a life is always the promise of
a greater good; the superabundance of the gift is the reality
of mercy because "the LORD will give what is good, and
our land will yield its increase" (Ps 85:12).

2.5. A Sacrament of the Indissoluble New Covenant, at the Heart of the "Divine Economy"

The context of the New Covenant, with direct reference
to marriage, clarifies its reality as a sacrament in the specific sense of a real sign of the union between Christ and
the Church (cf. Eph 5:32). The definitive character of the
New Covenant in Christ, including its requirement of per-
fection, therefore pertains to Christian marriage as such.

On the sacramental level, this central reality of Christianity was expressed by the unrepeatable character of some
sacraments, to the extent to which they signify an irrevocable choice of God (cf. Rom 11:29), beyond any contrary
moral behaviors that man may put into practice. Grace is
stronger than weakness, and it remains as a constant call
to conversion. The basis of this is baptism, the real sign
of this covenant that remains forever, even after the sin of
apostasy.

Mercy in this context signifies the constant possibility
of living according to the requirements of the Gospel.
The supremacy of God's grace is such that it goes beyond

human awareness and any type of judgment about oneself and one's own abilities. Ecclesial mercy must proceed from divine mercy according to its internal logic. The reality of grace at the baptismal font denies the claim that there are exceptions to the moral law justified by the consideration that it is impossible for man to live out its requirements.

> It would be a very serious error to conclude ... that the Church's teaching is essentially only an "ideal" which must then be adapted, proportioned, graduated to the so-called concrete possibilities of man, according to a "balancing of the goods in question." And of *which* man are we speaking? Of man *dominated* by lust or of man *redeemed by Christ*? This is what is at stake: the *reality* of Christ's redemption. *Christ has redeemed us!* This means that he has given us the possibility of realizing *the entire* truth of our being; he has set our freedom free from the *domination* of concupiscence.[47]

The divine economy is the way in which God draws man to himself; therefore it takes up into itself all the temporality inherent in the human condition. "[*Oikonomia* or] economy means the entire order of salvation of God as the benevolent father of the household and a spirituality that is marked by praise of the Church's all-merciful 'steward' or 'householder' and by trust in the 'good shepherd' who knows and calls each and every one by name."[48]

---

[47]John Paul II, Encyclical Letter *Veritatis splendor*, no. 103 (hereafter cited as *VS*); italics in original.

[48]Bernard Häring, *No Way Out? Pastoral Care of the Divorced and Remarried* (Middlegreen: St. Paul Publications, 1990), p. 40. Compare with Kasper, *Gospel of the Family*, pp. 50–51: "*Oikonomia* is not primarily a matter of a canonical principle, but rather a spiritual and pastoral basic attitude that applies the gospel like a good paterfamilias, understood as *oikonomos*, in conformity to the model of the divine economy of salvation."

There can be no concept with more pastoral importance than this one; surely, it has to be joined with the truth of revelation, which must be viewed in terms of the logic of love.[49] There is a very different concrete consideration of this principle of matrimony in the Orthodox churches, as we will see later.

Indissolubility does not result from a divine mandate that is added to marriage, but rather is a quality of the personal union that is established; *"the good of indissolubility is the good of marriage itself;* and the lack of understanding of its indissoluble character constitutes the lack of understanding of the essence of marriage."[50] The Western tradition spoke about the indissoluble bond that joins the spouses as a clear manifestation of God's transcendent action in matrimony—the reality of grace of "what God has joined together". The Council of Trent adopts this terminology to express the essence of this sacrament.[51]

---

[49] See *LF* 27: "Love is itself a kind of knowledge possessed of its own logic."

[50] "Address of John Paul II to the Prelate Auditors, Officials and Advocates of the Tribunal of the Roman Rota", January 28, 2002, no. 4; emphasis in original.

[51] See Council of Trent, Session 24 (November 11, 1563), can. 5 (DH 1805): "Si quis dixerit, propter haeresim, aut molestam cohabitationem, aut affectatam absentiam a coniuge dissolvi posse matrimonii vinculum: anathema sit" (If anyone says that the marriage bond can be dissolved because of heresy or difficulties in cohabitation or because of willful absence of one of the spouses, let him be anathema); and can. 7 (DH 1807): "Si quis dixerit, Ecclesiam errare, cum docuit et docet, iuxta evangelicam et apostolicam doctrinam, propter adulterium alterius coniugum matrimonii vinculum non posse dissolvi, et utrumque, vel etiam innocentem, qui causam adulterio non dedit, non posse, altero coniuge vivente, aliud matrimonium contrahere, moecharique eum, qui dimissa adultera aliam duxerit, et eam, quae dimisso adultero alii nupserit: anathema sit." (If anyone says that the Church is in error for having taught and for still teaching that in accordance with evangelical and apostolic doctrine [cf. Mt 5:32; 19:9; Mk 10:11ff.; Lk 16:18; 1 Cor 7:11], the marriage bond cannot be dissolved because of adultery on the part of one of the spouses and that neither of the two, not even the innocent one who has given no cause for infidelity, can contract another marriage during the lifetime of the other; and that the

The Second Vatican Council made this terminology its own while adopting a personalist perspective that in no way contradicts this terminology: "This sacred bond no longer depends on human decision alone",[52] and therefore it defines it as indissoluble.[53]

In order to explain the continuity of the marital covenant beyond a possible rupture due to sin, medieval theology resorted to the concept of the *res et sacramentum*, which is directly connected to the character of the sacraments that cannot be repeated. In this regard let us recall the words of *Familiaris consortio*: "The spouses participate in it as spouses, together, as a couple, so that the first and immediate effect of marriage (*res et sacramentum*) is not supernatural grace itself, but the Christian conjugal bond, a typically Christian communion of two persons because it represents the mystery of Christ's incarnation and the mystery of his covenant."[54] The union endures even if the spouses are unfaithful and do not live out this grace.

The reality of the bond has a personal character and is imprinted by the nature of the sacrament as the direct action of God, in order to guarantee the permanence of this union. In this way, the juridical good of the stability of marriage, which must be protected by law, is now a *sacramental* juridical good that the Church must preserve. It is part of the grace and faithfulness that leads into the New Covenant.

husband who dismisses an adulterous wife and marries again and the wife who dismisses an adulterous husband and marries again are both guilty of adultery, let him be anathema.)

[52] *GS* 48.

[53] See *GS* 50, where it states that marriage by "its nature" is "an indissoluble compact between two people".

[54] *FC* 13.

God's great gift of his mercy upon marriage grants the ability to overcome the human "hardness of heart" and to live in a truly indissoluble relationship. This grace is essential for those who are experiencing separation, so that they might understand that there is always the possibility of faithfulness and pardon. This has particular relevance in the case of separated Catholics who should be helped in their situation by the community,[55] while instead many times they feel abandoned.

It is clear, therefore, that any sort of spousal relationship apart from this bond will always be an unfaithful relationship and, for that very reason, adulterous. Christ's words are categorical: "Whoever divorces his wife and marries another, commits adultery against her; and if she divorces her husband and marries another, she commits adultery" (Mk 10:11–12).[56] There is no room for mercy in persistent infidelity, even if the person has repented of having caused it. Likewise, it is not possible to accept mercifully someone who remains in apostasy, nor someone who does not return to the marital covenant sealed by God, much less someone who is living in a way that contradicts it. This is

[55] See Livio Melina, "Quando la verità si incontra con la misericordia: comunità cristiana e famiglie separate", in Paolo Gentili, Tommaso and Giulia Cioncolini, eds., National Office of the Italian Episcopal Conference for the Pastoral Care of Families, *Luci di speranza per la famiglia ferita: Persone separate e divorziati risposati nella comunità cristiana* (Siena: Cantagalli, 2012), p. 85: "Pastoral ministers ought to reflect more on the condition of those who are separated, recognizing that it is a legitimate state of life and providing specific spiritual paths of reconciliation, aimed at reestablishing, when possible, conjugal life together, and in any case promoting fidelity to the sacramental bond."

[56] The same teaching is found in the Fathers of the Church; see Henri Crouzel, "Divorce et remariage dans l'Église primitive: Quelques réflexions de méthodologie historique", *Nouvelle Revue Théologique* 98 (1976): 903: "le nouveau mariage est constamment qualifié d'adultère." (The new marriage is constantly described as adulterous.)

not about denying the possibility of pardon, as the Novatians did, but rather about understanding that pardon can be granted only in the case of true repentance that alters the sinful situation. It is clear that adultery can be pardoned, but it is equally true that this cannot be the only sin that can be pardoned without repentance.

It is a contradiction in terms to establish a *salvific economy* that in fact denies the sacramental value of the union between a husband and a wife, or that accepts some *modus vivendi* apart from this sacramental character. That would mean accepting the notion that the economy inaugurated by Christ is transitory, or that we must wait for another one, or denying that it is universal, since only in that way could a person voluntarily exclude himself from it. The Christian believer continues to be a sinner, yet from the beginning the reply to this observation has been the return to the baptismal font, to repentance; this, however, was never understood as a new baptism with all the effects thereof. Reconciliation is renewing the covenant that persists as a source, not finding a different path for a supposedly Christian life apart from the New Covenant.

2.6. Its Importance in the Life of the Church

The rejection by the Catholic Church of the Orthodox practice is not due to various concepts of laxism or rigorism, but rather to a more developed sacramental concept that coincides precisely with medieval reflection, on the basis of which the treatise on the sacraments was elaborated in much greater depth. This is what was proposed without reservations to the Orientals in the two Councils aimed at union, namely, the Second Council of Lyons (1274) and the Council of Florence (1442).[57] The most explicit references that tend to forbid any sort of union whatsoever after separation are found in the profession of faith proposed to Michael Paleologus during the first of these councils.[58]

The nature of the sacraments is what guided the Church's pastoral reflection, in the sense that she does not have plenipotentiary authority over them. She received the sacraments from her Spouse and is the *administrator* of them, and not the proprietress; consequently, "no one questions the indissolubility of a sacramental marriage that was contracted and consummated (*ratum* and *consumatum*)",[59] a statement that John Paul II called defined doctrine: "It seems quite clear then that the non-extension of the Roman Pontiff's power to ratified and consummated sacramental marriages is taught by the Church's Magisterium as a doctrine to be held definitively."[60] The topic cannot be framed as a mere dispensation on the part of the hierarchy, because that would be an excessively juridical and nonsacramental view of the nature of the Church.

Any change that may be introduced in order to resolve the status of the divorced and remarried must clarify in the first place the profound meaning of the sacrament of

[57] See Council of Lyons II, Session 4 (July 6, 1274), *Profession of Faith of Michael Paleologus* (DH 860); Council of Florence, *Exultate Deo* for the Armenians (November 22, 1439), DH 1310–27.

[58] See Council of Lyons II, Session 4, DH 860: "De matrimonio vero tenet, quod nec unus vir plures uxores simul, nec una mulier permittitur habere plures viros." (As regards matrimony, she holds that neither is a man allowed to have several wives at the same time nor a woman several husbands.)

[59] *Gospel of the Family*, p. 43.

[60] "Address of the Holy Father John Paul II to the Tribunal of the Roman Rota", January 21, 2000, no. 8.

matrimony, which is quite special and, indeed, is part of the doctrinal patrimony of the Church. To propose a variation on the question therefore requires very profound doctrinal discernment; any attempt to conceal it or to assign secondary importance to it is contrary to the Church's tradition in a crucial aspect of the faith.[61]

Certainly, there are many new questions to study, since for many years now matrimony has been considered only marginally in comparison with the other sacraments. A renewed appreciation for the mysteric dimension of the sacraments, which goes beyond apologetics concerning the moment of their institution, has enabled theologians to explore new and very promising approaches, which the Synod can take into consideration as it revisits the topic of pastoral care of the family. Matrimony is a unique sacrament by virtue of the roots that it sinks into the order of creation and its value as a witness to the redemption of the heart that makes it possible.[62]

2.7. The Grace of the Indissoluble Bond as Source of Life

The path that we have traced is very different from the one that Kasper points to in his booklet, especially in the appendices, among other reasons because of his peculiar way of setting forth the history of the sacrament of

[61] One of the most significant theological shortcomings of the book by Bernard Häring on pastoral care for the divorced is that he does not mention this argument at all, presenting the matter merely as a question of pastoral compliance.

[62] See José Granados, *Una sola carne en un solo espíritu: Teología del matrimonio* (Madrid: Palabra, 2014).

matrimony, or because he discusses the Orthodox view of sacramental economy in a way similar to Häring's. This may be why his way of discussing the marital bond is very weak and actually tends to call it into question. This is precisely one of the aspects that an Orthodox theologian like Pavel (Paul) Evdokimov categorically disdains, while clearly referring to indissolubility: "The indissolubility of the bond is of no interest whatsoever to love. The problem arises when there is nothing more to salvage: the bond, which was initially declared to be indissoluble, has already dissolved and the law can do nothing to replace the grace: it can neither heal nor revive."[63] Kasper's words raise a similar doubt: "One ought not understand this teaching as a kind of metaphysical hypostasis beside or over the personal love of the spouses; on the other hand, it is not totally absorbed in their affective, mutual love, nor does it die with it (GS 48; EG 66)."[64]

It is true that in his book on marriage, Kasper seeks to provide a personalist explanation of the marital bond when he says: "Man and woman [i.e., husband and wife] are able to find their definitive status in this faithfulness. They become 'one flesh' or 'one' (Gen 2:24; Mark 10:8; Eph 5:31); in other words, they become a 'we' person. The marital bond of faithfulness creates something that transcends the single person and binds the history of two people definitively and at the deepest level together."[65] Nevertheless, when he has to describe its value in the

---

[63] Pavel Evdokimov, *Sacramento dell'amore: Il mistero coniugale alla luce della tradizione ortodossa* (Sotto il Monte Bg: Servitium, 1999), p. 244.

[64] *Gospel of the Family*, p. 16. The citation from *Evangelii gaudium* refers only very indirectly to the topic in question.

[65] Walter Kasper, *Theology of Christian Marriage*, trans. David Smith (New York: Seabury Press, 1980), p. 22.

context of a specific polemic about the divorced, every-thing seems to remain shrouded in ambiguity, since he concludes: "None of these statements can, it is true, be made purely objective. The phenomena to which they point can be interpreted in many different ways and are ultimately dependent on a definitive interpretation."[66]

This last nondefinition remains open to Häring's inter-pretation, which Kasper seems to adopt. In his pastoral treatment, Häring followed very closely what was said rather radically about divorce, from an Orthodox per-spective, by the theologian Evdokimov. The Russian author, drawing an analogy with death, which ends a marriage, proposes the following list of ways in which the bond can be "broken": "the death of the very *matter* of the sacrament of love by adultery; *religious* death by apos-tasy; *civil* death with a prison sentence; *physical* death *by absence*."[67]

Contrary to what Kasper declared at first, namely, that the bond does not die with the mutual affection, in the writings of the two authors that we have just cited there seems to be such a thing as the *death* of a love; this is a departure from the idea of the divine seal that, like fire, cannot be quenched by deep waters and is the pivotal point of the revelation of the Song of Songs (see Song 8:6).[68]

[66] Ibid., p. 23.

[67] Pavel Evdokimov, *Le Sacrement de l'amour: Le mystère conjugal à la lumière de la tradition orthodoxe* (Paris: Editions de l'Èpi, 1962), p. 256. Bernard Häring, for his part, speaks about physical death, moral death, psychological death, and civil death (see Häring, *No Way Out?*, pp. 41–49). He cites no source.

[68] See P. Ricoeur, "La metafora nuziale", in André LaCocque and Paul Ricoeur, *Come pensa la Bibbia: Studi esegetici ed ermeneutici*, ed. Franco Bassari (Brescia: Paideia, 2002), p. 269: "The true conclusion [of the Song of Songs] is found in 8:6.... The important thing here is not carnal consummation, which is never described or recounted, but rather the promise of the covenant, indi-cated by the 'seal', which is the soul of all things nuptial."

Ultimately, the Cardinal seems to maintain that something of the sacrament remains, because he (unlike the Orthodox churches) recognizes that another marriage cannot be celebrated. To be precise, he maintains very clearly that "the indissolubility of a sacramental marriage and the impossibility of contracting a second sacramental marriage during the lifetime of the other partner is a binding part of the *Church's faith tradition*."[69] Hence the "non-rigorist" solution would be to allow and tolerate a second union, which however would not be sacramental. Thereby, in his opinion, indissolubility would be preserved;[70] now therefore it is a question of understanding the new marriage in its natural, imperfect goodness, although in his view it is sufficiently acceptable. This is important in understanding how Kasper will envisage the pastoral solution in such a way that, in his opinion, dogmatic indissolubility is not compromised. The problem is that he does so precisely by going against the definitive character of the economy of Christ that is expressed in the sacraments. It is very odd to posit two orders of marriage in the ecclesial community:

[69] *Gospel of the Family*, p. 26; emphasis added.

[70] See Kasper, *Theology of Christian Marriage*, 69–70: "Many Christian theologians and pastors—including myself—believe that the facilities for pastoral help are insufficient in the present situation and that not enough provision is made for them in canon law as it stands now. Generally speaking, they do not advocate, of course, that a second marriage should receive a liturgical blessing or be solemnized sacramentally, thus putting it on the same level as the first marriage." Earlier he explained this in reference to the Oriental practice: "In the Eastern Church, for certain objective reasons which were based on a loose analogy between adultery and death, it became normal practice to permit remarriage, in accordance with the principle of economy, although the second marriage was not placed on the same level as the first. This practice does not violate the principle of indissolubility as such. What it does in fact is to provide the Christian who is ready to do penance, on the basis of God's mercy, with a new possibility of a human and Christian life within the Church in certain difficult situations" (pp. 56–57).

one for the perfect that is sacramental, and another for the imperfect, which is merely natural. This certainly is a way of undervaluing the action of grace in our hearts!

The Cardinal's last resort is to speak about the imperfect participation of *all* marriages in the union between Christ and the Church.[71] In reality, this last argument is extremely weak. There are various degrees of imperfection and one of them is the sin of injustice. If the bond is a loving relationship that demands justice, any act that is opposed to it would be an *unacceptable* imperfection, which cannot be the object of mercy until there is repentance for it and a real change of the situation that is contrary to the bond.

Naturally, before any discussion of this topic, it is necessary to recognize clearly what the practice of the Orthodox churches in this area actually is. There is no hiding the fact that in most cases it comes down to a simple dispensation obtained by paying a fee to the bishop's chancery, whereupon the Orthodox bishop automatically signs the permission for a second or a third marriage. This is something that the Catholic bishops and priests living in those countries experience daily; in practice it very clearly presupposes a divorce, something utterly foreign to the idyllic vision that the Cardinal presents: "The path in question

---

[71] See ibid., p. 80: "All human will to marriage is therefore an imperfect realization of the mystery of Christ and his Church, which strives to realize itself more and more perfectly. This may therefore be particularly important if, for one reason or another, a sacramental church marriage is not possible, but a will to marriage, which is both human and Christian, is really present, as is frequently the case with those who have divorced and are remarried. Such partners should trust in God to give them the grace to fulfill their duties as a married couple, since their union is a participation in the mystery of Christ and the Church because of the faith, which is expressed as penance for their guilt incurred in the breaking of their first marriage."

would not be a general solution. It is not the broad path for the great masses, but a narrow path for the indeed smaller segment of divorced and remarried individuals who are honestly interested in the sacraments."[72] We will discuss this aspect in greater depth in the chapter of this present book on pastoral care.

2.8. An Ecclesial Understanding

The preceding brief discussion clearly shows the importance of the essential truths of revelation that are at stake in this matter. Surely, we find ourselves deeply involved here in one of the central theological elements of the Christian kerygma (proclamation), and a balanced understanding of it is fundamental for the real life of the Church.

Therefore, based on our presentation, there seems to be no room for a simple "pastoral solution" along the lines of tolerance. Inasmuch as this concerns our very understanding of the bond, this is not something that can be allowed in some cases, but rather is an aspect that affects the life of *all* marriages, which experience the indissoluble bond as a source of grace, a source of new strength to confront difficult moments, proof of the true sacramental presence of Christ in their lives. To transform it into something else, to debase it to a simple common responsibility between the spouses, would be an enormous blow for all Christian marriages. This is such an important question that it must be made absolutely clear, above and beyond simple pronouncements that nothing will change.

[72] *Gospel of the Family,* pp. 32–33; emphasis added.

Therefore it is necessary to seek true firmness in our statements, as is only right with everything that has to do with the central nucleus of the kerygma. In this sense, we understand that it is difficult to make such an important question depend simply on a theological argument such as the one that we have presented, although we have sought to make it rigorous and, naturally, it is based on the very clear recent Magisterium. The Church's tradition is a necessary reference point in determining accurately how the question has been understood and whether there is more basis for the Orthodox "economic" tolerance than we have attributed to it in these pages. We need to see whether there is room for recognizing the Orthodox discipline and whether doing so could lead to a change in the Latin Church's doctrine about the bond.

Therefore, it is absolutely necessary to refer to the Church of the Fathers. We will discuss this topic in the following chapter.

3

The Experience of the Primitive Church: Faithfulness to the Gospel of the Family

"The current situation of the church is not unique. Even the church of the first centuries was confronted with concepts and models of marriage and family that were different from that which Jesus preached."[1] The historical parallel that Cardinal Kasper proposes here is of great interest and very timely. It has a twofold value: cultural and normative. It refers to the way in which the Church responded to a cultural challenge from the beginning of her history, teaching us to do the same in our days, as we showed in chapter 1. At the same time, it is a normative parallel, since it shows how these first Christian communities received the revelation of Christ, and how they expressed in their life the concrete way of interpreting what the Bible tells us about the gospel of the family.

This is vital in the case of marriage, which, as a historical institution, is at the mercy of cultural changes and, in particular, of the sexual revolutions that have punctuated history. In this day and age, we ought to learn a lot about how the Church evangelized the family at those moments.

In the primitive Church that emerged from the Jewish context, there were three aspects of the confrontation with

[1] *Gospel of the Family*, introduction, p. 2.

the Hellenistic world with respect to marriage. In the first place, Christian believers found themselves in a society with a high divorce rate that greatly influenced them; since their way of acting appeared strange to others and on all sides, they were rebuked by a different model of behavior. Moreover, many of them had converted and came from very diverse situations; some, in fact, were divorced, and it was not easy for pastors to determine what the necessary requirements were for receiving baptism. Finally, the bishops had to respond to new situations in the absence of a previous tradition that might help them to evaluate each factor deliberately, since it made no sense for them to refer either to Jewish or to Roman law.

Whereas the first question facing the Church of the Fathers was very similar to ours, the other two are profoundly different—in particular with regard to the fact that our present-day differentiation between civil and religious marriage did not exist, and the sacramental aspect of marriage was not very well defined as to its essence and what differentiates it from natural marriage.[2] This aspect must be kept clearly in mind when we consult the characteristic testimonies, if we want to learn from them how to respond to the cultural challenges of our time.

3.1. A Constructive, Ecclesial Vision

Before proceeding with a more detailed view of the arguments adopted and debated, it is necessary to clarify

---

[2] See Tomás Rincón, *El matrimonio: misterio y signo* (Pamplona: EUNSA, 1971).

one principle: in dealing with these texts, we must not seek to corroborate our own opinion, but rather to learn from a way of acting. It is necessary to observe the testimonies as a whole and not focus *exclusively* on those that favor a predetermined attitude. The evaluation of the texts depends on the genre to which they belong, which varies depending on whether we are reading a letter, a homily, an exegetical commentary, a canon with juridical force, and so forth. Within the context of the works by the same author, we cannot isolate one text; rather, it is necessarily to evaluate it with respect to his teaching as a whole. Here we have, then, a series of fundamental criteria for proceeding constructively, and not *apologetically*. There is no sense turning to these writings if one does so with an obvious prejudice. In that case, one does not learn from them, but utilizes them for a predetermined purpose. It is necessary to refer to these principles, since in many treatises on marriage they have not been taken into consideration. Indeed, there have been cases of outright manipulation.[3]

Furthermore, as far as the Synod is concerned, the perspective must be *ecclesial* if it is to be of help in discernment. Therefore it must not foster polemics but rather understand that this is a matter that affects the whole Church and that it must be discussed with due precision and wisdom. As we saw in the preceding chapter, we are facing a question that pertains to the *faith of the Church*; therefore, we must seek the foundation of this faith also in the practical

[3] Exemplary for its clarity and rigorous historical scholarship along these lines is the discussion by Henri Crouzel, "Divorce et remariage dans l'Église primitive: Quelques réflexions de méthodologie historique", in *Nouvelle Revue Théologique* 98 (1976): 891–917.

interpretation thereof in the primitive Church. For a matter of such great importance, it is not enough to present a vague *attitude* of the Fathers of the Church, since in its formal flexibility it could give rise to any sort of subjective interpretation whatsoever; instead, we can seek several points in common that might help us to act in an ecclesial manner.

In particular it is necessary to avoid a harmful strategy that has already caused enough grief for the Church: the strategy aimed at *sowing doubt*, without providing convictions. It is very easy to open up a breach in a conviction so as to destroy it. We have seen this done in many moral questions on the societal level, with devastating results. Within the Church, we cannot resort to this methodological suspicion, nor can we allege that it is appropriate to allow certain practices *ad experimentum* in such a delicate question, since we have also seen that, in the end, one does not derive a different teaching from any practice that has positive and negative effects. Ultimately we must recall the moral principle that when there is any doubt, before acting in conscience it is necessary to resolve it as much as possible, for the purpose of attaining sufficient *moral certainty* to act. This is what Saint Alphonsus Liguori correctly declared[4] in order to distance himself both from a simple probabilism[5] (which regards a lesser doubt

[4] See Saint Alphonsus Maria de Liguori, *Theologia Moralis* I, Tract. 1, c. 2, no. 22 (Rome: Typographia Vaticana, 1905), p. 11: "numquam esse licitum cum conscientia practica dubia operari." (It is never lawful to act with a practical conscience in doubt.)

[5] See *Theologia Moralis* I, Tract. 1, c. 3, no. 55, p. 25: "Nam ad licite operandum sola non sufficit probabilitas; sed requiritur moralis certitudo de honestitate actionis." (For in order to act lawfully, probability alone is not sufficient, but rather moral certitude about the decency of the act is required.)

as reason to act) and the absolute application of a tutiorist certitude.

In order to justify an important change in ecclesial practice that concerns doctrine, it is altogether insufficient to cite the mere *doubt* that it may be possible to act differently, based on several past experiences. This is not an adequate way of approaching the writings of the Fathers.

3.2. An Erroneous Assertion by Cardinal Kasper

The criteria listed above lead us to evaluate Kasper's address (and the texts added to it for the publication of his booklet) with respect to the primitive Church as altogether *one-sided*, based on unfounded assertions, some of them plainly exaggerated. Although the Cardinal's expository style always tends to present two positions, so as then to make a synthesis of them, in this case his choice of texts, his way of interpreting them, and the historical thread that he proposes fall into the error just mentioned.

But that is not all: even though the reasoning of this theologian and the sources that he cites follow those in his earlier book *Theology of Christian Marriage* almost to the letter, strangely enough, in his booklet we note a radicalization of the attitude of ecclesial tolerance toward divorced and remarried individuals. To prove this, just compare its overall approach to the topic through the evaluation of the patristic testimonies that describe a tolerant practice in the primitive Church.

In his book on marriage, the theologian Kasper asserted: "A relatively flexible practice in the Church is evident from the statements made by some of the Fathers, at least with regard to those who had married again after a divorce in which they were the innocent party."[6] This statement very cautiously intends to introduce several testimonies, extremely few in number, which refer to a certain tolerance in these situations. It clearly indicates, moreover, that they do not refer to marriages that simply failed, but to a particular case that is distinct from the others: the case of an innocent person abandoned by his own spouse. The perspective of the Cardinal's address to the Consistory is quite different, since he asserts: "So much is nevertheless certain, that in individual local churches there existed the customary law, according to which Christians, who were living in a second relationship during the lifetime of the first partner, had available to them, *after a period of penance*, admittedly no second ship—no second marriage—but indeed a *plank of salvation* through participation in communion."[7] This assertion is more favorable to that practice, which he now describes as "certain"; thus he gives the impression that the texts presented afterward cite this tolerance positively. Kasper adopts an even stronger position in the second excursus of his booklet, where he concludes by saying: "There can, however, be no doubt about the fact that in the early church there was, according to the customary law in many local churches, the praxis of pastoral tolerance, clemency, and forbearance after a period of penance."[8] Now it says that there was no doubt and that this was a practice in *many* local churches. In other words, this establishes almost as a norm what at first was viewed simply as a possibility.

---

[6] Walter Kasper, *Theology of Christian Marriage*, trans. David Smith (New York: Seabury Press, 1980), p. 54.

[7] *Gospel of the Family*, p. 31; emphasis added.

[8] Ibid., p. 37.

In reality, after reading the texts, at most one might cautiously want to qualify them as "several testimonies to a certain flexibility". The evident change that takes place between the one and the other moment of our theologian's life seems to be due to the fact that in the latter case it was necessary to support a concrete proposal at the Consistory—in other words, an apologetic argument.

By adopting this new line of argument, it becomes very easy for the Cardinal to conclude: "The Orthodox churches preserved the pastoral point of view of the early church tradition, in accordance with their principle of *oikonomia*."[9] This expression of unbroken continuity between the patristic tradition and Orthodoxy contrasts with what is presented as a substantial change of the West with respect to the Church's initial position: "The Western church went a different way.... One can ask whether juridical perspectives, which occur very late in history, are not being one-sidedly pushed into the foreground."[10]

It is necessary to clarify this assertion. On the one hand, it is an oversimplification of the Western tradition, since it is due not merely to the assignment of priority to some juridical terms; on the contrary, the *sacramental* value of matrimony was explored in much greater depth with contributions of great theological significance, which have no counterpart in the Eastern theology of that period.[11] One cannot dismiss the juridical consequences that resulted from this development, which was fundamentally *theological* in a tradition that, in these beginnings, did not separate pastoral practice, theology, and law.

[9] Ibid., pp. 37–38.
[10] Ibid., p. 38.
[11] Just think of the monumental work by Hugh of Saint Victor in *De Sacramentis christianae fidei* (Münster: Monasterii Westfalorum, 2008).

In this sense, it must be declared with certainty that it is a *serious historical error* to claim that the current practice of Orthodox *oikonomia* had its proper origins in a hypothetical patristic tolerance. A serious historical study shows that, with regard to divorce, the juridical tradition of the Orthodox churches results from *pressure by the Byzantine emperors.*[12] The Cardinal refers only summarily to this historical fact, presenting it only at the level of examples of cases in which to apply a tolerance that is already well consolidated,[13] whereas instead it must be seen as a real variation of the concept that involved the hidden acceptance of divorce. In fact, this occurs with a certain awareness of *change and not of continuity* in the Orthodox churches themselves. After objective research, it must be said that the history of Eastern theology shows that it was precisely the imposition of a political and juridical practice that prompted Byzantine theologians to seek precedents that would allow them to justify such a novelty.[14] This novelty,

[12] For a decisive, well-documented study, see Luigi Bressan, *Il divorzio nelle Chiese orientali* (Bologna: EDB, 1976).

[13] Cf. *Gospel of the Family*, p. 38: "However, since the sixth century, following Byzantine imperial law, they have gone beyond the position of pastoral tolerance, clemency, and forbearance and they recognize—besides the provisions concerning adultery—additional grounds for divorce, which are based on the moral and not only the physical death of the marriage bond." Although the first way of presenting it seems to be critical, the mention of the analogy of the "moral death" of a marriage, which as we saw is taken from Pavel Evdokimov, appears with no qualification, whereas it requires explanation, since this is an improper analogy (see Pavel Evdokimov, *Le Sacrement de l'amour: Le mystère conjugal à la lumière de la tradition orthodoxe* [Paris: Editions de l'Èpi, 1962]). This aspect is clarified in the response to Basilio Petrà, who, for his part, adopts this position; see Ángel Rodríguez Luño, "L'estinzione del matrimonio a causa della morte: Obiezioni alla tesi di B. Petrà", in *Rivista di Teologia Morale* 130 (2001): 237–48. Petrà responds in Basilio Petrà, "Risposta a Rodríguez-Luño", in *Rivista di Teologia Morale* 130 (2001): 249–58.

[14] For this view of the history of theology, see Gilles Pelland, "Le dossier patristique relatif au divorce: Revue de quelques travaux récents (2)", in *Science et Esprit* 25 (1973): 99–119.

which began in Byzantium, only gradually spread to the other Orthodox churches. In other words, it springs from a desire to extend political power over the Church, by means of a Caesaro-papist concept, which is altogether foreign to any evangelical principle or to any truly theological idea of *oikonomia*. This must be stated clearly out of respect for historical accuracy, which is essential for such a difficult topic, but also for pastoral conscientiousness, since nowadays there are no emperors—although there is no lack of power centers that are very interested in imposing their views on the Church, in one way or another.

3.3. The Texts Presented

This little volume has no other purpose than to seek to clarify the terms somewhat, for the sake of a sufficiently deliberate debate, as is only fair after a public intervention in which the question was broached. This is why, in this context, we will limit ourselves to discussing the texts cited by Cardinal Kasper in order to put them in the proper context and then interpret them.

Of course, as we have shown repeatedly, on the whole, the argument implied in the Cardinal's presentation gives voice only to those texts that serve his objective: showing that in the early Church tolerance for the reception of Communion by the divorced and remarried was accepted and widespread. In doing so, he disregards one obvious fact: the number of patristic texts that categorically deny this possibility is much higher, and these passages are more frank and clear than the excerpts that the Cardinal cites. In order to conduct an objective scholarly study, in order to reconstruct an overview and draw reliable conclusions, it is necessary to present the whole and not just details.

It is true that we must always remember the importance of admitting an exception to the general rule; nevertheless, in order to assess the authentic context of the patristic era, we must observe that Christians were conscious of adopting a position that was in striking contrast with the world that surrounded them, and that a Christian's witness through his own marriage was very important. This confers a particular historical authenticity to the patristic arguments, which are quite different from simple Roman law or the customs of the day, even though there was an awareness of the influence that they exerted on the faithful.

Canon 8 of the Council of Nicaea

Let us start with the Nicene canon, since it appears in the address to the Consistory almost by way of conclusion: "There was, therefore, a pastoral practice of tolerance, clemency, and forbearance, and there are good reasons for assuming that this praxis was confirmed by the Council of Nicaea (325) against the rigorism of the Novatianists."[15] But that is not all: the Cardinal also cites the Council in excursus 2 of his booklet in a footnote (p. 40, n. 20), so as to make its content quite clear.

Among the bibliography listed, he also cites *Divorzio, nuove nozze e penitenza nella chiesa primitiva* (*Divorce, New*

---

[15] *Gospel of the Family*, p. 31. Kasper refers again to this canon in the second excursus of his booklet (p. 37), although in a more nuanced way, as a mere possibility, clarifying that the canon is opposed to rigorism and not in favor of the practice in question: "It is against the background of this practice that canon 8 of the Council of Nicaea (325), which was directed against the rigorism of Novatian, [should perhaps] be understood." (The English translation reads "must surely"; the Italian, *va forse*.)

Marriage and Penance in the Primitive Church) by Giovanni Cereti,[16] whose interpretation of this canon views it as very clearly accepting divorced-and-remarried individuals into complete communion in the Church. The reference to this book is not insignificant, since Cereti's interpretation is artificial and radically apologetic, constantly manipulating the terminology and the sources. For an example of Cereti's lack of rigor, just look at how he treats the canon of Saint Epiphanius,[17] which should be considered parallel to the one of Nicaea and the best way of interpreting it. From the outset, he does not use the critical edition, which would have allowed him to clarify the terms of the problem, but rather the one that he considered more useful for his purposes.[18]

Since Cardinal Kasper cites the Council's text in the footnote, it does not appear to be superfluous to reproduce it here the way he did: when they convert to the Catholic Church, "so-called pure ones [i.e., the Cathari, the Novatians] ... must foster community both with those who live in a second marriage as well as with those who lapsed during persecution."[19] The text that he refers to, actually, was translated somewhat differently in the standard edition of Church documents, the Denzinger-Hünermann, an

[16] Giovanni Cereti, *Divorzio, nuove nozze e penitenza nella chiesa primitiva* (Bologna: EDB, 1977). Cited in excursus 2 of *Gospel of the Family*, p. 36; the fact that, at least in the Italian version of his booklet, Kasper cites all three editions of Cereti's book (2nd ed., 1988; 3rd ed., 2013) shows the importance attributed to this book. Cereti had previously introduced the topic generically in Giovanni Cereti, *Matrimonio e indissolubilità: nuove prospettive* (Bologna: EDB, 1971).

[17] See Cereti, *Divorzio, nuove nozze e penitenza*, pp. 371–79.

[18] See the subsequent debate about the critical text conducted by P. Nautin, "Divorce et remariage chez saint Épiphane", in *Vigiliae Christianae* 37 (1983): 157–73; Henri Crouzel, "Encore sur divorce et remariage selon Épiphane", in *Vigiliae Christianae* 38 (1984): 271–80.

[19] First Council of Nicaea, canon 8, quoted in *Gospel of the Family*, excursus 2, p. 40, n. 20.

edition which the Cardinal explicitly refers to in the Italian version of his text without following it even there. It reads: "With respect to those ... who call themselves 'the Cathars' ... it is fitting that they profess in writing ... to remain in communion with *those who have been married twice* and with those who have lapsed during persecution".[20]

The text is indeed relevant, not only because it refers directly to "those who have been married twice" (*dígamoi*), but also because the canon intends to refute a *rigorist* position like that of the Novatians, who denied sacramental pardon for some sins. The text would certainly be widely recognized because of its authority, since it was issued by the first ecumenical council! In order to explain the force of such a conciliar requirement, it would be necessary to presuppose an extended practice of full acceptance of these persons into ecclesial communion in the Church as a whole. Moreover one would have to recognize in the canon the exemplary character of the principle from which the requirement is derived: the Church, in this Council, upheld tolerance while opposing an unacceptable rigorism. It is the action of a Church that admits sinners, in contrast with a so-called church of the "pure" (Cathari) that rejects those who do not fulfill its own requirements, which are sometimes inhumane.

Nevertheless, clarifying the terminology of this well-known fact is extremely helpful in putting these two statements into the proper context, and, as a result, the obstacles to understanding it are removed. This text is a formula of *retractatio*, a reconsideration within a *canon* that

[20] Heinrich Denzinger-Peter Hünermann, *Enchiridion Symbolorum: Compendium of Creeds, Definitions and Declarations on Matters of Faith and Morals* (San Francisco: Ignatius Press, 2012), p. 52, n. 127, emphasis added.

has juridical force; its intent is to require what is considered to be the indispensable minimum. In order to understand the contents of such a *retractatio*, it is necessary in the first place to know what the Novatians taught; otherwise the terms will be interpreted without adequate context. The term *digamoi* is in itself very generic (as is confirmed by the disparity of the translations that it gives rise to), so much so that only the context of the canon and the subsequent interpretation of it can assign a full meaning to it. We must not forget, however, that in patristic writings the term never refers indistinctly to individuals who are widowed and have entered a second marriage and to the divorced and remarried.

Unfortunately, Cereti does not follow this very logical path[21] and takes another that is altogether artificial. His argument is so simple that it can be summarized in three steps: (1) this is about some rigorists who deny the forgiveness of sins; (2) the three most serious sins of that era were apostasy, adultery, and murder; (3) hence, there is an obligation to admit those who commit these sins, and consequently adulterers, into the Church without any other considerations. This would necessarily include, in his view, the divorced and remarried. Within the context of his argument, one cannot help pointing out that nothing more is said about murder, since few were guilty of murder and it was not a pastoral problem.[22]

Only one thing is important. This is where he concentrated all his efforts, and it should be highlighted, since I think that it influenced Kasper's approach: "Our

[21] Namely, the one spelled out in Henri Crouzel, "Les digamoi visés par le Concile de Nicée dans son canon 8", in *Augustinianum* 18 (1978): 541–45.

[22] Cf. Cereti, *Divorzio, nuove nozze e penitenza*, p. 300.

investigation will be limited to only one problem: Was the Church convinced or not that she could absolve any sin whatsoever?"[23] With this initial perspective, Professor Cereti frames the question as though it were a debate between the rigorists and the merciful, without looking at what is behind the Church's practice in both cases of reconciliation with the Church, namely, a truth of the faith about the sacramental value of baptism and of marriage, which must guide her action, with regard to penance as well. The apostate has not ceased to be baptized and called to union with God; the adulterer can be pardoned insofar as there is repentance and further situations are avoided. This is a fundamental principle that seems to be obscured when we think only in terms of rigorism or tolerance, since the conclusion then is based not on a truth but only on subjective dispositions, and obviously that ends up dividing the Church.

Because he adopts an initial prejudice, in his extensive research into the sources on the Novatians he concentrates only on what interests him: the denial of pardon for the sin of adultery, and on this point he piles up one text after another. In contrast, he does not consider the evidence of their radical rejection of the second marriages of widows as something that came into conflict with the Catholic Church.[24] This attitude was in keeping with the rigorism typical of North Africa, which was strongly influenced by

[23] Ibid., p. 325.
[24] See especially the statement by Socrates in *Historia ecclesiastica* 5. 22 (PG 67:641; NPNF-2 2:132b–133a): "The Novatians in Phrygia do not admit such as have twice married; but those of Constantinople neither admit nor reject them openly, while in the Western parts they are openly received." Cited in ibid., p. 311.

Tertullian, yet the author insists on considering it to be of little or no importance. Furthermore, for lack of a rigorous methodology, Cereti sets aside any further mention of the Novatians at Nicaea, whereas such references would have to be taken into consideration precisely in order to demonstrate the way in which the Fathers—who already were acquainted with this canon—interpreted it, as well as how it was in fact then implemented in practice in the Church. It is absurd to think that such a forceful requirement of tolerance would have left no subsequent traces, even with regard to knowledge about Novatian's supporters. Without getting into an excessively technical discussion, just recall that Saint Augustine describes the Novatians's view as a *heresy*. In this instance the Doctor of Grace is not referring to a form of rigorism, but rather to the rejection of something that is part of the Church's faith. His words are all too clear: he refers to them as heretics with respect to *only two questions*, the ones that appear in the canon of Nicaea, and he uses quite similar terminology: "The Cathars, who very proudly and very odiously call themselves by that silly name on account of their purity, do not allow second marriages and reject penance, following Novatus the heretic, and so they are also called Novatians."[25] Their separation from the Catholic Church cannot be reduced to the point of their denial of penance (moral rigorism), since we must not forget their wrong understanding of marriage (heresy concerning sexuality). This is a very different way of interpreting Nicaea.

[25] Translated from the Latin: Saint Augustine, *On Heresies* 38 (NBA, XII/1:90–91): "Cathari, qui seipsos isto nomine quasi propter munditiam superbissime atque odiosissime nominant, secundas nuptias non admittunt, paenitentiam denegant, Novatum sectantes haereticum, unde etiam Novatiani appellantur."

In order to understand that this is a question about faith and not just about pardoning certain sins, we can turn to Saint Augustine's letter to the widow Juliana, in which he insists on the state of widowhood: "For, even as the good of holy virginity, which thy daughter hath chosen, doth not condemn thy one marriage; so neither doth thy widowhood [condemn] the second marriage of any[one]. For [this reason], specially, the heresies of the Cataphryges and of the Novatians swelled, which Tertullian also, inflated with cheeks full of sound not of wisdom."[26] He is clear, therefore: this negation was explicitly part of a doctrine in which the Novatians separated themselves from the Catholic Church; but he explains the difference with equal clarity: "For adultery and fornication are evils."[27] There is no doubt, therefore, that the contrast with the Novatians consists in the admission of the second marriage of widows.

Cereti, on the contrary, never once admits that this sect tried to impose *absolute monogamy* by demanding that a layperson not enter a second marriage after being widowed—a requirement that did apply, though, to clerics. He refers instead to a series of absurd considerations, such as a prohibition imposed on clerics to remarry after a divorce.[28] All this, just to assert that the term "bigamist", at Nicaea, refers to the second marriage of a divorced individual that is fully accepted in the Church.

---

[26] Saint Augustine, *On the Good of Widowhood* 4.6 (NPNF-1 3:443a). "Non damnat unas nuptias tuas, sic nec viduitas tua cuiusquam secundas. Hinc enim maxime Cataphrygarum ac Novatianorum haereses tumuerunt, quas buccis sonantibus, non sapientibus etiam Tertullianus inflavit."

[27] "Mala sunt enim adulterium vel fornicatio" (ibid.).

[28] Cereti, *Divorzio, nuove nozze e penitenza*, p. 318.

In reality, what Nicaea confirms is a *legal canon*, not a pastoral one, which intends to define the conditions for accepting the Novatians who wish to be reintegrated into the Catholic Church. The minimum requirement, therefore, is their acceptance of second marriages of widowed individuals, a practice that is nevertheless mentioned in Scripture (see Rom 7:3; 1 Cor 7:9), but it is implausible to think that it refers to a practice that, according to all the references—including the ones that we will see in a moment—met with no approval in the Church and was a topic of debate. If one were to accept Cereti's interpretation, one would have to conclude that the present-day Catholic Church was Novatian and would have to retract its errors if it was to be admitted to communion with the Church of Nicaea.

Cereti was explicitly criticized in the book published by the Congregation for the Doctrine of the Faith on the reception of Holy Communion by divorced-and-remarried individuals,[29] particularly in the document published to declare the unlawfulness of the procedure that the bishops of the Upper Rhineland, Kasper among them, had promoted in a pastoral letter. Certainly the Cardinal was not unaware of these serious critiques of Cereti, and we wonder why he would have suggested him as a serious source on this topic. It is true that he declared publicly, in a letter that appeared in the newspaper *Die Tagespost*, that

---

[29] See Gilles Pelland, "La pratica della Chiesa antica relativa ai fedeli divorziati risposati", in Congregation for the Doctrine of the Faith, *Sulla pastorale dei divorziati risposati* (Vatican City: Libreria Editrice Vaticana, 1998), 99–131. The author explicitly discusses Cereti's book on pp. 115–21. In the next few passages citations will be based on Pelland's translations, since they are more rigorous than other more colloquial translations.

his position differs from this one, and we are glad about that, but he ought to tell us where the difference lies, since what he says about the interpretation of canon 8 of Nicaea has no other source than the Italian theologian.[30]

Origen's Comment about the Matthean Exception

The text of Origen's comment about the Matthean exception is the second most important, since the Cardinal employs it to express the logic of tolerance that must be accepted. He refers to it twice in his booklet, the second time more explicitly, since he asserts: "This customary law is expressly attested to by Origen, who considers it not unreasonable (*Commentary on Matthew*, 14:23).... And some others also refer to it. They justify the 'not unreasonable' statement with the pastoral intention of 'preventing something worse'."[31]

It seems to us worthwhile to cite in full the passage in question:

Contrary to *Scripture*, some leaders of the Church have allowed a second marriage to a woman whose husband was still alive. They did this despite what *is written*: "A wife is bound to her husband as long as he lives" (1 Cor 7:39), and "a married woman ... will be called an adulteress if

---

[30] In favor of his position, Cardinal Kasper also cites an article by Joseph Ratzinger, which, however, does not speak about the Council of Nicaea; on top of this, the author himself has since explicitly distanced himself from the position he had advanced in this article (cf. Joseph Ratzinger, "Church, Pope and Gospel", in *The Tablet* 245 [October 26, 1991], pp. 14–15). Kasper might have wanted to mention this.

[31] *Gospel of the Family*, excursus 2, p. 37. The other reference is in the text of his address, p. 31: "Origen reports on this custom and describes it as 'not unreasonable'."

she lives with another man while her husband is alive"
(Rom 7:3). Nevertheless they did not act entirely without
reason (οὐ μὴν πάντη ἀλόγως). Probably this weakness
[*symperiphora*, indulgence] was permitted in consideration
of greater evils, contrary to the original law reported by
the *Scriptures*.[32]

It is indeed surprising that Kasper has always carefully
avoided citing the complete passage, in which Origen
three times clarifies that this is a practice *contrary to Scripture*, which he considers as the highest authority.[33] Consequently, the testimony given by Origen about this practice,
which in his view is unlawful, absolutely cannot be considered as agreement with the aforesaid tolerance. Taken in
its entirety, indeed, the passage is particularly enlightening.
Their way of acting is regarded with some understanding: "they did not act entirely without reason" (*ou mēn
pántē alógōs*). Nonetheless, this is different from saying that
what they do is "not unreasonable". Instead, Origen really
simply recognizes the existence of some reason (it is not
totally irrational), derived from a human logic, which must
be inserted into a higher logic coming from Sacred Scripture. Along these lines, the "greater evils" themselves can
be understood as referring to worse transgressions that make
these seem less irrational,[34] and not necessarily to evils that

[32] See Pelland, "Pratica della Chiesa", pp. 106–7; emphasis added. The original text is found in PG 13:1245–46.

[33] See Henri Crouzel, *L'Église primitive face au divorce* (Paris: Beauchesne,
1971), p. 83: "Three times he underscores the fact that they acted in this way
contrary to Scripture: despite the moderate tone, the rebuke is clear, since for
him Scripture is the highest norm."

[34] This is insinuated by Crouzel in ibid., pp. 83–84: "They allowed this liai-
son or this weakness, or employed this indulgence, so as to avoid greater evils.
These are therefore attenuating circumstances which do not eliminate his basic
disapproval."

would result if they were not tolerated. Consequently from this passage emerges something quite different from what is suggested as a matter of principle by Kasper's address as it is written, and of course this makes his method of citation unacceptable. Similarly, his digression on avoiding "greater evils" proves to be inadequate without a consideration of the evil that in fact occurs.

Actually, the Cardinal uses it as a summary of the reason for all pastoral tolerance when he says: "Out of pastoral concern 'to prevent something worse,' these fathers were willing to tolerate something that, in itself, is unacceptable."[35] Therefore it is easy, for the Cardinal, to turn this into a proposal for the contemporary life of the Church, based on a merely consequentialist approach:

> The path in question would not be a general solution. It is not a broad path for the great masses, but a narrow path for the indeed smaller segment of divorced and remarried individuals who are honestly interested in the sacraments. Is it not necessary precisely here to prevent something worse? For when children in the families of the divorced and remarried never see their parents go to the sacraments, then they too normally will not find their way to confession and communion. Do we then accept as a consequence that we will also lose the next generation and perhaps the generation after that? Does not our well-preserved praxis then become counterproductive?[36]

Any tolerance of an evil by someone in authority is rooted in the fear of worse consequences, but in the Church's

---

[35] *Gospel of the Family*, p. 31.
[36] Ibid., pp. 32–33.

case there is no denying the injustice that this implies—that is to say, the reality of a sin—and there is no suspending its consequences.

Saint Basil's Canon

Let us turn now to Saint Basil's canon, one of the texts currently being debated the most, since it undoubtedly speaks directly about tolerance with regard to a divorced-and-remarried individual. Indeed, this was precisely the text adopted by the Orthodox canonists to justify their praxis.[37]

Here is what the passage says: "The charge here affects her who dismissed her husband—according to the cause for which she withdrew from marriage.... [The woman] who left is an adulteress if she went to another man. But, he who was abandoned is to be pardoned, and she who dwells with such a one is not condemned."[38]

Certainly this is a difficult passage; it speaks about excusing and not condemning, but it is not easy to understand the precise situation to which it refers. As for the woman who is not condemned, everything seems to indicate that this concerns a woman who is unaware of her husband's previous situation, as it proves to be the case later on.[39]

---

[37] Cf. Henri Crouzel, "Encore sur divorce et remariage selon Épiphane", in *Vigiliae Christianae* 38 (1984): 279; Pavel Evdokimov, *Sacremento dell'amore. Il mistero coniugale alla luce della tradizione ortodossa* (Sotto il Monte, Bergamo: Servitium Editrice, 1999), p. 251.

[38] Saint Basil, Letter 188, 9 (FOC 28:20); cf. Pelland, "La pratica della Chiesa", p. 113. Original text in PG 32:677–80.

[39] See Saint Basil, Letter 199, 46 (PG 32:738–39), where the Latin translation reads: "Quae viro ad tempus ab uxore derelicto insciens nupsit, ac deinde dimissa est, quod prior ad ipsum reversa sit, fornicata quidem est, sed

Therefore it is different from the excuse pertaining to the man, even though nothing is said about what specifically is being excused, whether the author means the sin of separation that allows of repentance, or the sin of a subsequent union that is considered understandable—although it is not described as lawful—or else the question of the ignorance that it involves, if connected with the fact of knowing nothing about the previous wife, not even whether she is still alive.[40] The passage leaves the readers rather perplexed, because in speaking about a form of tolerance it clarifies neither the terms nor the limits within which it unfolds. The context is a set of widely varied "canons" that deal with specific cases and are difficult to evaluate. It is something quite different from an established norm aimed at considering a divorced-and-remarried person as having a status that is accepted within the Church.

In any case, this particular advice must be understood within the context of an obvious rejection of any type of divorce, which the Cappadocian Father expresses unconditionally and with a clear sense of condemnation in another

---

imprudens." (The woman who unwittingly marries a man deserted at the time by his wife, and is afterward repudiated, because of the return of the former to him, commits fornication, but involuntarily [NPNF-2 8:239b].) It is incomprehensible why the Cardinal, in *Gospel of the Family* (p. 37), also cites Saint Basil, Letter 199, 18 (PG 32:719–20), which says: "Quemadmodum igitur eum qui cum aliena est muliere, adulterum nominamus, non prius admittentes ad communionem, quam a peccato cessaverit" (We call the man who lives with another man's wife an adulterer, and do not receive him into communion until he has ceased from his sin [NPNF-2 8:237a]), a passage that is clearly contrary to his position, rather than the other section of the letter that he usually refers to: "canon" 35 (PG 32:727–28) (NPNF-2 8:239a).

[40] All of these possibilities, with respect to the other "canons", are carefully considered by F. Cayré, "Le divorce au IVᵉ siècle dans la loi civile et les canons de saint Basile", in *Échos d'Orient* 19 (1920): 295–321.

work: "A man who has dismissed his wife is not permitted to marry another, nor may she who has been repudiated by her husband be married again with another."[41]

The tolerance, however, is not connected with a judgment that the marriage is lawful, but rather with the decision not to impose a set punishment.[42] In fact, the appropriate penance is the reason why the Bishop of Iconium asks Saint Basil for these "canons" or rules, which stylistically resemble a letter more than a legal document.[43]

The Mention of Gregory of Nazianzen

In the case of the mention of Gregory of Nazianzen we are looking at a marginal note, a comment made in passing, which in reality speaks only about the way in which

---

[41] Saint Basil, *Moralia*, reg. 73, 2; cf. Pelland, "Pratica della Chiesa", p. 115. The original text can be found in PG 31:851–52.

[42] Following is a summary of what could be deduced from a textual analysis from Pelland, "La pratica della Chiesa", pp. 114–15 (emphasis in original):

> *Objectively*, the woman in canon 46 fornicated by joining in marriage with an already married man, but *subjectively* we cannot blame her, because she did not know it. The woman in canon 9, for her part, was not unaware, and therefore we speak *a fortiori* about *objective* guilt. Likewise the woman in canon 46 will be able to marry another man after a "waiting period", since her first union was not a marriage. This is true also of the woman in canon 9, for she too was joined with an abandoned husband. Why should we suppose that there was a marriage in one case (can. 9) and not in the other (can. 46)?
>
> In short, it is not clear that canon 9 authorizes the second marriage of a man abandoned by his wife. An attentive reading of the texts suggests only that this testified to a certain indulgence in his regard: *he will not be subjected to penance as though there were no mitigating factors.*

[43] Cf. Pelland, "Pratica della Chiesa", p. 113: "The specific aim of these documents, as Basil notes in Letter 217, is to determine the penalties due to certain failings."

the Church Fathers understood the so-called Matthean exception or the exception "on the ground of unchastity" (Mt 5:32).[44] It was not understood as a reason for divorce and for being able to remarry, but rather as an imperative to separate because the wife was dissolute (which, however, included no permission to remarry). Let us look at Saint Gregory's exact words: "Now the Law grants divorce for every cause; but Christ not for every cause; but He allows only separation from the whore; and in all other things He commands patience."[45] He speaks therefore about a separation, but never about any permission for a second union. The argument from silence for this permission, in this case, is incomprehensible, since we see that *immediately* before this he says: "But if Christ is One, one Head of the Church, let there be also one flesh, and let a second [marriage] be rejected; and if it hinder the second, what is to be said for a third? The first is law, the second is indulgence, the third is transgression, and anything beyond this is swinish."[46]

We may think that this denial, stated along general lines, ends up allowing by way of "indulgence" the possibility of a second marriage for someone widowed by the spouse's death, but what is to be said about marriages that are directly opposed to Scripture? This is even truer if we recall that the Cappadocian Bishop declares that "divorce ... is entirely contrary to our law, though the Roman law may determine otherwise."[47]

---

[44] Cf. Henri Crouzel, "Le texte patristique de Matthieu V.32 et XIX.9", *New Testament Studies* 19 (1972–1973): 98–119.

[45] Saint Gregory of Nazianzen, Oration 37.8 (NPNF-2 7:340b).

[46] Ibid., NPNF-2 7:340a-b.

[47] Saint Gregory of Nazianzen, Letter 144 (NPNF-2 7:480b), cited in Pelland, "La pratica della Chiesa", p. 117.

The Possible Exception of Saint Augustine

The last patristic reference that we find in the address cites Saint Augustine, none other than the Church Father to whom is attributed the concept of the marital bond as indissoluble. If this author, notwithstanding his rigid view, admitted some exceptions, why not do so now?

Let us look at the words of this Doctor of the Church: "In the actual divine utterances there is a similar uncertainty as to whether such a person, who is certainly allowed to divorce the adulteress, is nevertheless to be regarded as an adulterer if he remarries, especially as the fault in that case would, in my view, be a venial one."[48]

The text is cited because it describes a divorce as "venial", although the Augustinian terminology about "venial" sins is very complex and would imply at least some doubt, given his ironclad position against the acceptance of any marriage after divorce.

The interpretation changes when we look at the context for this qualification, namely, the case of *admitting a divorced catechumen to baptism*,[49] in other words, someone married twice *before* baptism. Augustine's position, which is to accept the candidate on certain conditions that assure that he was not to blame for the divorce, presupposes therefore a particularly sophisticated understanding of the difference between divorce among catechumens and

[48] Saint Augustine, *On Faith and Works* 19.34 (ACW 48). Original text: (CSEL 41/5:81): "et in ipsis divinis sententiis ita obscurum est utrum et iste, cui quidem sine dubio adulteram licet dimittere, adulter tamen habeatur si alteram duxerit, ut, quantum existimo, venialiter ibi quisque fallatur."

[49] He says so immediately afterward: "For this reason those who are manifestly sinners by unchastity must absolutely be excluded from baptism" (ibid.). Original text in CSEL 41/5:81: "Quamobrem quae manifesta sunt impudicitiae crimina, omni modo a Baptismo prohibenda sunt."

marriage between baptized parties that was by no means common in that era.[50]

Once again, what emerges from an analysis of the text is quite different from what the Cardinal would have us suppose in his address.

Conclusion

The importance of referring to the Fathers of the Church is twofold, and from this twofold perspective we should present the conclusion to our rapid explanation.

As for the attitude of the primitive Church with regard to the question of divorce in a society where the extent of this phenomenon was very similar to ours, we see that the way of confronting it contains a juridical value within the Church, which is expressed precisely at the moment when the institutional development of the Church is beginning. The interventions always tend to judge the situation objectively, differentiating among cases and providing *objective* guidelines in a sense that is also canonical.

Along with this perspective, the path for pastoral care to follow was defined; based on truly fundamental arguments, it tended toward a practical consensus centered on

---

[50] This is the explanation given by the commentators; see J. Pegon, "Notes complémentaires", in *Oeuvres de Saint Augustin, Première série. VIII: La foi chrétienne*, "Bibliothèque Augustinienne" (Bar le Duc: Desclée de Brouwer, 1982), p. 508: "The only point where he displays some originality, it seems, in the direction of indulgence, is the solution that he gives for cases of a concubine who has broken up and of a husband who has dismissed his wife after she has been convicted of adultery, but without remarrying afterward.... Such broadmindedness, which was by no means common at the time, reveals not only his kindly soul, but above all a rare doctrinal reliability."

arguments that would be capable of serving as the foundation for principled pastoral activity.

In reality, if we review all the testimonies on the question, it is surprising to observe the *scarcity* of references to any sort of tolerance. The cases allowing the most leeway have to do with very concrete, particular situations and fit into a very severe penitential approach that included, as the usual condition, abstinence from sexual relations. In view of an environment that was so prone to divorce, the truly rare position of tolerance is an important lesson about the way in which the question was considered— not as a secondary matter, but rather as something very important with respect to the Gospel and which therefore had to be defended forcefully because of the enormous pressure that Christians had to withstand. The witness of their concrete stance of defending indissolubility, in opposition to the societal customs of that era, was a realization of the prophetic value of Christian marriage that changed the society of that time.

A Life Given in Time:
Rebuilding the Moral Subject

4.1. The Capacity to Make and to Keep Promises

Cardinal Kasper beautifully explains that the teaching concerning the indissoluble bond of marriage "is good news, that is, definitive solace and a pledge that continues to be valid. As such it takes the human person and his or her freedom seriously. It is the dignity of the human person to be able to make permanent decisions."[1] Nowhere else does this ability to make permanent decisions find a clearer expression than in the capacity to make and to keep promises. It is here that human freedom is most clearly actualized. To see the greatness of this capacity and its relation to freedom, one does not need to be a believer. In his work *The Genealogy of Morals*, Friedrich Nietzsche, who is under no suspicion of being a Christian apologist, sings the praises of the person who is able to promise. For Nietzsche it is here that we have the case of the sovereign individual, who has "his own independent, enduring will, the man who is *entitled to make promises*. And in him we find a proud consciousness, tense in every muscle, of what has

[1] *Gospel of the Family*, pp. 16–17.

finally been achieved here, of what has become incarnate in him—a special consciousness of power and freedom."[2] The "liberated man, who is really *entitled* to make promises, this master of *free* will", is the "the owner of an enduring, indestructible will".[3] What distinguishes him from other people is that he "gives his word as something which can be relied on, because he knows himself strong enough to uphold it even against accidents, even 'against fate' ".[4] It is certainly true that in these phrases we do not find a drop of creaturely humility, an inkling of human frailty, or the slightest notion of our human need for healing grace. They are not written with a Christian attitude, for which our merits are themselves God's gifts. And yet, though overconfident in human strength, here Nietzsche calls an excellence an excellence and as such expresses a profound truth of high relevance for our present days.

People today often think that to make a lasting commitment in an irrevocable promise means to delimit or to lose one's freedom. In the words of Benedict XVI, they ask, "Can one bind oneself for a lifetime? Does this correspond to man's nature? Does it not contradict his freedom and the scope of his self-realization? ... Is lifelong commitment antithetical to freedom?"[5] Nietzsche's

---

[2] Friedrich Nietzsche, *The Genealogy of Morals*, trans. Douglas Smith (Oxford: Oxford University Press, 1998), p. 41.

[3] Ibid.

[4] Ibid. For a very elucidating discussion of this passage, see Hannah Arendt, *The Human Condition,* 2nd ed. (Chicago: University of Chicago Press, 1998), p. 245: "Nietzsche, in his extraordinary sensibility to moral phenomena, and despite his modern prejudice to see the source of all power in the will power of the isolated individual, saw in the faculty of promises (the 'memory of the will,' as he called it) the very distinction which marks off human from animal life."

[5] "Address of His Holiness Benedict XVI on the Occasion of Christmas Greetings to the Roman Curia", December 21, 2012.

response would certainly be that the contrary is the case: through promising we actualize our freedom, taking hold of our future. By binding our will, we become masters of it, emancipating ourselves from the winds of passion, the fluctuations of chance, and even the strides of fate. The person who is truly free can promise, and only the person who can promise is truly free. Hence, Benedict and Nietzsche would probably agree that "man's refusal to make any commitment" is "a result of a false understanding of freedom and self-realization as well as the desire to escape suffering".[6]

The question that remains is thus not whether promising is contrary to freedom—which it is not—but whether promising is something that is within our reach. Was Nietzsche not overconfident in human power? If it were a question of human power just by itself, the answer would probably have to be that indeed he was. The good news of the Gospel, however, is precisely this: God is giving his people a new heart, one which enables them to be faithful to the covenant that God offers them and to which they respond precisely by making promises—their baptismal vows for all Christians and then their marital or religious vows according to the personal vocation of each.

4.2. The Problem of Invalid Marriages

With all this in mind, let us now turn to discuss the first of the two approaches that Cardinal Kasper proposes toward resolving the problem of the divorced and civilly

[6] Ibid.

remarried. He writes, *"Familiaris Consortio* says that some of the divorced and remarried are subjectively convinced in conscience that their irreparably broken, previous marriage was never valid (FC 84). Many pastors are in fact convinced that many marriages, which were concluded in ecclesial form, are not validly contracted."[7] According to him, we can no longer make the general assumption that a given marriage is valid, an assumption that to his mind has become a legal fiction. Given the presumably high incidence of invalid marriages, the Cardinal asks "whether the juridical path, which is in fact not *iure divino* [by divine law], but has developed in the course of history, can be the only path to the resolution of the problem, or whether other, more pastoral and spiritual procedures are conceivable".[8] In fact, "one might imagine that the bishop could entrust this task to a priest with spiritual and pastoral experience as a penitentiary or episcopal vicar."[9]

Here, Cardinal Kasper offers a concrete proposal about modifying a procedure that it is within the Church's authority to change. The present juridical procedure possibly leading to a declaration of nullity is not part of divine revelation, and hence one may certainly discuss ways of improving it. And yet, there may be good practical reasons for disagreeing with the Cardinal's proposal, such as, for instance, those that he himself adduces just a few lines further down, where he emphasizes that "it would be mistaken to seek the resolution of the problem in a generous expansion of the annulment process. The disastrous impression would thereby be created that the Church is

[7] *Gospel of the Family*, p. 28.
[8] Ibid.
[9] Ibid.

proceeding in a dishonest way by granting what, in reality, are divorces."[10] It is not clear how these two passages are compatible with each other. It can hardly be denied that a procedure in which it is no longer an ecclesial court but an individual priest who judges on the nullity of a marriage precisely represents the "generous expansion of the annulment process", that Cardinal Kasper himself confesses to be undesirable because of the disastrous impression it could create.

As is, it is already difficult enough to explain to people that annulment is not a Catholic divorce. From Saint John the Baptist to the English Martyrs and beyond, the Church knows of witnesses who have shed their blood in defense of the sanctity of the marital bond. What would a simple penitentiary vicar have done in the face of Henry VIII's request? In the sixteenth century, the Church essentially lost an entire nation because of her firm insistence on the indissolubility of marriage. Should we in the least suggest today that this was imprudent, or is there not a higher logic that forbids even the semblance of compromise when it comes to the deposit of faith entrusted to the Church by God himself? Thus, Cardinal Kasper has himself indicated the reasons that speak against his proposal. And yet, something still more fundamental needs to be said about his suggestion.

We must wonder how the affirmation that "many pastors are in fact convinced that many marriages, which were concluded in ecclesial form, are not validly contracted"[11] could be adduced to be the solution of anything. If the conviction of many pastors turns out to be really true,

[10] Ibid., p. 29.
[11] Ibid., p. 28.

it cannot possibly be considered as a path to a partial resolution of the problems connected with the divorced and civilly remarried. *It is itself the major problem.* We need to see things in their proper perspective. As Cardinal Kasper rightly points out, only the "smaller segment of divorced and remarried individuals" is "honestly interested in the sacraments".[12] The question of admitting the divorced and civilly remarried to Communion is hence a problem that concerns only few of the faithful. It is a problem that has arisen in the cultural context of the West and is perceived to have a certain urgency only there, while the local churches in Asia and Africa may well have quite different concerns. Besides, as we have seen, Saint John Paul II and Benedict XVI have already offered feasible solutions, in *Familiaris consortio* (no. 84) and *Sacramentum caritatis* (no. 29), respectively. So a new pastoral solution would concern only those of the divorced and civilly remarried who are desirous to receive the sacraments *and* who are not inclined to follow the indications laid out by the Church thus far. To refer to the presumed fact that a vast number of sacramental marriages contracted today are invalid as a solution to the problem of admitting a small number of the divorced and remarried to the sacraments is to present a major predicament as the solution of a minor difficulty.

In other words, the "solution" refers to a crisis that is of a far more fundamental nature than the problem it is meant to resolve. It is one thing to embark on a life project and encounter difficulties and even failures, which may then lead to separation and even civil divorce. It is yet quite another thing to experience oneself deprived of the very

---

[12] Ibid., p. 33.

capacity to embark on a project in which one can succeed or fail, and nothing less is implied when we speak of
invalid attempts at contracting marriage. Thus, the more
important question for the pastoral care of the family today
is *how to assure that marriages are contracted validly* and not
how to find additional ways of admitting to Communion
the divorced and remarried who do not wish to walk the
paths already laid out by the Church.

4.3. The Human Being in Modernity: Made a Camper through Divorce

To indicate the direction in which a response can be found
to the critical question of how to assure that marriages are
contracted validly, we will need to take a look at today's
crisis of the moral subject. Why do people find it so difficult to promise, that is, to make commitments that bear on
their whole lives? The Polish sociologist Zygmunt Bauman has found a highly suggestive image to describe the
human person in modern times, namely, that of a camper
at a caravan site. "Drivers bring to the site their own homes
attached to their cars and equipped with all the appliances
they need for the stay, which at any rate they intend to be
short."[13] Campers are autonomous, aware of their rights,
and at the same time not too much interested in working
for the good of the place they are visiting:

> Since they pay, they also demand. They tend to be quite
> adamant when arguing for their rights to promised services

[13] Zygmunt Bauman, *Liquid Modernity* (Malden, Mass.: Polity Press, 2000), p. 24.

but otherwise want to go their own ways.... If they feel short-changed or find the managers' promises not kept, the caravanners may complain and demand their due—but it won't occur to them to question and renegotiate the managerial philosophy of the site, much less to take over the responsibility for running the place.[14]

If campers do not like a site, they will move on. They have no ambition to invest time and labor into improving the place. In a similar way, modern individuals tend to think they have all they need within themselves. If they are dissatisfied with their cities, their workplaces, or their intimate relationships, they are little inclined to attempt to make things work. Their instinctive reaction, rather, will be to move on. For Bauman, one of the roots of this mentality are the changed working conditions. While in the age of the first Ford factory—the age of "heavy modernity"—there was "a 'till death us do part' type of marriage vow between capital and labour",[15] flexibility has become the new creed of our own day's "liquid modernity". Work life has become episodic and the readiness to leave it all behind and start anew is by now an absolute necessity for whoever desires to continue having a professional occupation. It is only too tempting to apply this model to human relationships.

On top of this, our modern-day means of production have become so powerful that the only limits to production seem to be the limits of consumption. This is what Hannah Arendt suggests when she says, "Under modern conditions, not destruction but conservation spells ruin

[14] Ibid.
[15] Ibid., p. 116.

because the very durability of conserved objects is the greatest impediment to the turnover process, whose constant gain in speed is the only constancy left wherever it has taken hold."[16] It is consumption that keeps the economy going, thus becoming the first virtue of the conscientious citizen, while thrift and saving are public vices, at least at the moment when we understand how the modern economy works. All too easily this mentality enters into human relationships. As Bauman points out, "Bonds and partnerships tend to be viewed and treated as things meant to be *consumed*, not produced.... If the partner in partnership is 'conceptualized' in such terms, then it is no longer the task of both partners 'to make the relationship work'—.... It is instead a matter of obtaining satisfaction form a ready-to-consume product."[17]

The sheer existence of the legal institution of divorce has done a lot to promote this attitude. Law has an educative effect. The mere fact that divorce legislation exists in secular society witnesses to the fact that the State authority—which for many people still is an authority even today—does not presume that marriage is meant to last "till death do us part", but that it is a temporal arrangement. A few years ago a local politician in Germany, Gabriele Pauli, caused a great stir by suggesting to limit the marriage commitment to seven years, which could then be renewed if the partners so desired.[18] The public disapproval that

---

[16] Arendt, *Human Condition*, p. 253.

[17] Bauman, *Liquid Modernity*, pp. 163–64.

[18] Cf. "Kampf um CSU-Vorsitz: Pauli will Ehen auf sieben Jahre befristen", *Spiegel Online*, September 19, 2007, http://www.spiegel.de/politik/deutschland /kampf-um-csu-vorsitz-pauli-will-ehen-auf-sieben-jahre-befristen-a-506669 .html.

Ms. Pauli earned for her proposal shows that people still have some sense of marriage as a natural institution that human beings enter, but do not create, an institution of marital love that by its nature lasts until the death of one of the spouses. And yet, there is nothing in the State's legal texts to justify any public indignation. There is hardly a *qualitative* difference between the legal possibility of obtaining a "little-" or no-fault divorce and the proposition to delimit the legally binding term of marriage to seven years.

The legal institution of divorce assumes that partnership is temporary, which, according to Bauman, "tends to turn into a self-fulfilling prophesy.... If people assume their commitments to be temporary and until further notice, these commitments do tend to become such in consequence of these people's own actions."[19] The mere fact that it is easily possible for people to have a divorce greatly contributes to their getting into situations where they think they need a divorce, since it changes the way they enter their relationships and the way they work or fail to work these same relationships. If people assume a permanent commitment, they will be more discriminate before entering it, and they will also invest more labor in trying to make it work once they have entered it. Every marital contract under the reservation of divorce, in contrast, implicitly views the partners' union with the same attitude that is made quite explicit in the practice of prenuptial agreements fashionable in some countries. Here the future spouses already agree on the conditions of a future divorce in case one or both of them desire to exit the relationship. How could anyone expect such a partnership to last? How

---

[19]Bauman, *Liquid Modernity*, p. 164.

could it not come to a premature end if this end has been
thought of and prearranged from the start? Is it not better
to be betrayed by one's friends than to mistrust them?[20] Is
any friendship, and especially a spousal one, possible if it
is marked by suspicion from the very beginning?

The Canadian sociologist Jacques T. Godbout states that
"divorce is probably the most important social revolution
of modern times."[21] The reason for this is that divorce has
significantly changed the husband–wife relationship from an
unconditional to a conditional type of bond. What distinguishes friends from family members is that the former are
chosen while the latter are not. We do not choose our parents, brothers, sisters, or children. The result is that family
relationships are less free than friendships, but more secure,
inasmuch as they are precisely unconditional. At any point
a friend can tell a friend that he considers their friendship
to be done with; at that moment it will indeed be over.
A father, at a point of distress and utter disappointment,
can tell his son, "You are no longer my son", and yet, his
son will still be his son. Hence "friendship cannot replace
the family."[22] There is of course one family relationship
that *is* freely chosen, and this is its founding nucleus: the
couple.[23] The idea of marriage in its full sense is that by
the marital covenant the two enter into an unconditional

[20] Cf. François de La Rochefoucauld, *Collected Maxims and Other Reflections*,
trans. E. H. Blackmore and A. M. Blackmore and Francine Giguère (Oxford:
Oxford University Press, 2007), Maxim 84, p. 27: "It is more shameful to mistrust our friends than to be deceived by them."

[21] Jacques T. Godbout, in collaboration with Alain Caillé, *The World of the
Gift*, trans. Donald Winkler (Montreal and Kingston: McGill-Queen's University Press, 1998), p. 34.

[22] Ibid.

[23] Cf. ibid.

relationship that is similar to all other family relations, turning two strangers into kin.[24] The relationship is freely chosen in its beginning like friendship but then, through the covenant, becomes unconditional like kinship. According to this line of thought, it is as absurd to tell one's wife that she is no longer one's wife as it is to tell one's sister that she is no longer one's sister, and it is as impossible to have an ex-husband as it is to have an ex-father.

A marriage agreement that allows for divorce is evidently of a very different kind: the relationship is freely chosen in its beginning and continues to be freely chosen in its duration. It is this difference that makes for a true social revolution, and which makes Godbout wonder whether "the unconditional nature of other family relationships (brothers, sisters ...) [will] survive the end of unconditionality in the couple".[25] Modernity risks leaving people isolated, without roots and without ties and ultimately abandoned. Thus, by defending the indissolubility of marriage, the Church does an invaluable service to mankind in the modern age. It would be disastrous if her pastors and teachers were to give the least impression of having come to terms with the fact that in most legislations in the world there exists the legal institution of divorce. It is a fact that she can never accept.[26] If she loves human beings, if she wants to help to rebuild the moral subject, she will always make clear her opposition to divorce and insist that for her the State has no more authority to define

[24] Cf. Scott Hahn, *Kinship by Covenant: A Canonical Approach to the Fulfillment of God's Saving Promises* (New Haven: Yale University Press, 2009).

[25] Godbout, *World of the Gift*, p. 34.

[26] Cf. Leo XIII, Encyclical Letter *Arcanum*, February 10, 1880. The teaching of the first encyclical letter entirely dedicated to the topic of marriage is still of relevance, today perhaps more than ever.

marriage as it has authority to define the law of gravity, and that therefore, by defining terms of divorce, it is overstepping its boundaries. Indeed, not too long ago, the position that it is not up to the discretion of the State to define what marriage is was not exclusive to the Church but was upheld also by thinkers not known to be fervent churchgoers. Thus, in an editorial for the *Rheinische Zeitung*, which he directed at the time, the young Karl Marx expressed himself in these terms about the question of the divorce bill: "The legislator ... does not *make* the laws, he does not invent them, he only formulates them, expressing in conscious, positive laws the inner laws of spiritual relations.... A person who contracts marriage does not *create* marriage, does not *invent* it, any more than a swimmer creates or invents the nature and laws of water and gravity."[27]

We have begun this chapter asking about how the Church's pastoral care can help people to invest themselves in a promise, to make lasting commitments, enabling them to contract valid marriages. A first answer would be to open up to the faithful a new perspective, emphasizing that the Church really believes in what she is saying. For some of her faithful the first time they hear about marital indissolubility may well be during the last encounter with the priest in marriage preparation. The engaged couple may be sincere; they may hear the words, and yet, for lack of a larger context, be confused about their literary genre. "Until death do us part"—isn't this a beautifully poetic way of expressing what one feels at the moment? By saying these words, what else could one mean but, "Yes,

---

[27] Karl Marx, "Der Ehescheidungsgesetzentwurf", *Rheinische Zeitung* 353 (December 19, 1842); English translation: Karl Marx and Friedrich Engels, *Collected Works*, vol. 1 (Lawrence and Wishart: London, 1975), p. 307.

right now I do feel like wanting to be with you for the rest of my life"? The idea that these words are more than an expression of one's momentary feelings, that they are the expression of a promise with which one commits one's will for one's entire future and gives a definitive form to one's life, may simply not be readily available to people growing up in our emotivist age. They will not be able to understand it, unless it is proclaimed with insistence and conviction.

If it is true that there is an immense amount of invalid marriages, then this is not a solution to anything, and a valid, indissoluble marriage is not a burden. The Church needs to do everything in her power to enable people to contract valid marriages, and part of this is to tell them clearly the truth about indissolubility. The pastors and teachers of the Church must not allow themselves to be tempted into thinking that this truth is burdensome, that for as long as people are ignorant, they are not culpable of their sins and can thus live a happy life without risking their eternal salvation.[28] Sin hurts—even in this life. It is

---

[28] Cf. Joseph Ratzinger, *On Conscience* (San Francisco: Ignatius Press, 2007), pp. 13–14:

In the course of a dispute, a senior colleague, who was keenly aware of the plight to being Christian in our times, expressed the opinion that one should actually be grateful to God that He allows there to be so many unbelievers in good conscience. For if their eyes were opened and they became believers, they would not be capable, in this world of ours, of bearing the burden of faith with all its moral obligations.... What disturbed me was the notion that it harbored, that faith is a burden which can hardly be borne and which no doubt was intended only for stronger natures—faith almost as a kind of punishment, in any case, an imposition not easily coped with. According to this view, faith would not make salvation easier but harder. Being happy would mean not being burdened with having to believe or having to submit to the moral yoke of the faith of the Catholic church.

precisely mercy that requires us to tell people the truth, certainly in view of their eternal salvation, but also in view of the happiness that can be had this side of heaven. The truth does not make this life harder but enables us to live it well. Life does not come with a manual, and particularly in the area of sexuality all human beings are highly vulnerable. Here, it is nothing short of cruel to let people learn by trial and error. It would mean to abandon them; it would mean to expose them to potentially dire consequences. Some errors are so devastating that it is enough to commit them just once for one's whole life to be wrecked. Of course, the guilt can always be forgiven, but some damage may well be humanly irreparable. By one mistake, what could have become a beautiful life can be completely destroyed, at least in its earthly dimension. This is why educators must not be afraid of taking responsibility, and in particular the Church needs to live up to the calling she has from God, that is, to tell them the good news, a gospel that touches their lives and calls them to conversion (cf. Mk 1:15). Finding renewed and more effective forms of marriage preparation, in particular of the remote and proximate preparation of which *Familiaris consortio* speaks (see no. 66), would thus seem to be among the most urgent challenges to the pastoral care of the family in the context of evangelization.

4.4. Committing One's Life in a Vision of Fruitfulness

How can we help today's "emotivist" moral subject, a person who is able to promise a feeling, but not a life? We have already spoken about society as a whole. Here the legal institution of divorce has a highly negative educative effect on people who are about to get married. It is one of the clearest expressions of the "culture of the provisory" of which Pope Francis has warned us.[29] A further important reason for why many persons today find it difficult to promise their whole lives to each other is because they do not manage to look at their lives as a whole. They view their lives as an accumulation of interchangeable episodes without any inherent unity. According to some authors, our present culture has fallen prey to a "chronological atomism", that is, "an understanding of life as composed of interchangeable and essentially identical units of time".[30] Forgetting that there is a life cycle made up of distinct phases may lead to bizarre situations. Thus, at one point Max Scheler recounts his strange encounter with an elderly man who behaved as if he were eighteen years old.[31] His was a case of a clinically attested mental illness. And yet many of our contemporaries live in an analogous way without literally having a mental problem. Their difficulty

[29] See "Address of Pope Francis to Engaged Couples Preparing for Marriage", February 14, 2014.

[30] President's Council on Bioethics, *Beyond Therapy: Biotechnology and the Pursuit of Happiness* (New York, N.Y.: Regan Books, 2003), p. 185.

[31] Cf. Max Scheler, "Repentance and Rebirth", *On the Eternal in Man* (New Brunswick, N.J.: Transaction Publishers, 2010), p. 45:

In a German lunatic asylum, some years ago, I came across an old man of seventy who was experiencing his entire environment on the plane of development reached in his nineteenth year. That doesn't mean that the man was still lost amid the actual objects making up his world when he was a boy of eighteen, that he saw his home of those days, with its attendant people, streets, towns, etc. No, he saw, heard and experienced nothing but what was going on around him in the room, but he lived it all as the boy of eighteen he once was, with all that boy's individual and general impulses and ambitions, hopes and fears.

rather lies in their tendency to see life as a random sum of disparate parts, while instead life is more like a symphony, where each part, precisely in its difference from all the others, is related in a meaningful and quasi-necessary way to the whole, making the whole beautiful.[32]

Many of our contemporaries lack the idea that they are not the simple administrators of whatever happens to come their way but that they are the artists of their lives. To be an artist, to build one's life, one needs a project. To have a project, one needs a goal. We would like to suggest that it is here that we can find one of the core reasons for many modern persons' inability to promise: they no longer perceive an aim or end that would give meaning to their lives as a whole. As Pope Francis beautifully puts it, "Promising love for ever is possible when we perceive a plan bigger than our own ideas and undertakings, a plan which sustains us and enables us to surrender our future entirely to the one we love."[33] Essentially, people have lost the idea of love's fruitfulness. Jesus tells his disciples what we are entitled to believe he tells every human being: "I chose you and appointed you that you should go and bear fruit that your fruit should abide" (Jn 15:16). Any composite reality derives its unity from its end or aim. Life can have a unity only if it has a purpose, an end, or goal. Jesus tells us that this purpose is fruitfulness, and prior to the modern age his words would have been self-evident to any reader or listener. There is more to life than just living. If there is nothing we desire more than living, then soon enough we will begin to loathe living. There is

[32] Cf. President's Council on Bioethics, *Beyond Therapy*, p. 185.
[33] *LF* 52.

hardly anything that people, and especially young people, desire more in their lives than a mission, something to live and possibly to die for. Until recently it was very clear to people that this noble striving was naturally related to the family. Recognizing oneself as a son or daughter, one appreciates and accepts the original gift of life. Responding in gratitude to the gift of life that one has freely received, one becomes aware of a calling to pass this life on in love: to become husband and wife who together are called to become father and mother.[34] For most people it is in the family that they begin to live for others, that they begin to respond to their innate vocation to a common life lived in a love that is fruitful. Even for those who receive the call to continence for the sake of the Kingdom, this fundamental structure remains intact. They too are called to fruitfulness. It is not only the pleasures of intercourse that they renounce for the Kingdom. They also renounce their earthly fruitfulness: to have a family and to have children of their own. Jesus' promise to them is a superabundant recompense precisely to *this* renunciation; theirs will be an abounding spiritual fruitfulness: "Truly, I say to you, there is no man who has left house or wife or brothers or parents or children, for the sake of the kingdom of God, who will not receive manifold more in this time, and in the age to come eternal life" (Lk 18:29).

By separating sexuality from any idea of fruitfulness, the sexual revolution has trivialized sex, closing off the idea

[34] Cf. "Address of His Holiness Benedict XVI to Participants in the Meeting Promoted by the Pontifical John Paul II Institute for Studies on Marriages and Family", Friday, May 13, 2011: "It is in the family that the human person discovers that he or she is not in a relationship as an autonomous person, but as a child, spouse or parent, whose identity is founded in being called to love, to receive from others and to give him or herself to others."

that human sexuality has anything to do with the human person's most fundamental calling, that is, with the very meaning of his life. And yet, there is no casual sex. Every time a man and a woman unite in the flesh, they also unite in their inmost souls. A spiritual bond is created that will last a lifetime, as casual as the encounter may be: "[H]e who joins himself to a prostitute becomes one body with her" (1 Cor 6:16). Detached sex is anthropologically impossible. People become most seriously attached to the ones they have sex with. Every time human beings change sexual partners, the previous partners take part of them with them, and thus people eventually become detached from themselves. The changing of sexual partners fragments people. To this effect, the sociologist Jay Teachman presents statistical data suggesting that women who have their first experience of sexual intimacy with the person who is or will become their marital partner have a lower risk of marital failure than those who have had previous sexual encounters with other partners.[35] He highlights that according to his findings a woman's premarital sex or cohabitation with her future husband does not seem to

[35] See Jay Teachman, "Premarital Sex, Premarital Cohabitation, and the Risk of Subsequent Marital Dissolution among Women", *Journal of Marriage and Family* 65 (May 2003): 444–55:

Women who cohabit prior to marriage or who have premarital sex have an increased likelihood of marital disruption. Considering the joint effects of premarital cohabitation and premarital sex, as well as histories of pre-marital relationships, extends previous research. The most salient finding from this analysis is that women whose intimate premarital relationships are limited to their husbands—either premarital sex alone or premarital cohabitation—do not experience an increased risk of divorce. It is only women who have more than one intimate premarital relationship who have an elevated risk of marital disruption. This effect is strongest for women who have multiple premarital coresidental unions. (p. 453)

increase the risk of subsequent marital failure and suggests that this data speaks in favor of accepting pre-premarital sex and cohabitation as acceptable cultural practices.[36] It is difficult to see, however, how this interpretation can follow from the facts described. When a man and a woman come together intimately before they are married, even if they are serious about their relationship or already engaged, they precisely don't know yet that their present partner will certainly be their future spouse. If he turns out ultimately not to be the future spouse, one can say that according to the research results, the future marriage with a different partner will suffer from a serious liability.

Teachman's study suggests that the first sexual encounter in particular creates an especially strong bond. This is very well expressed in the otherwise almost unbearably nihilistic film *The Great Beauty (La Grande Bellezza)*, by Paolo Sorrentino. Jep Gambardella, the main character, portrayed by Toni Servillo, spends his completely fragmented life hopping from flower to flower, looking for the Great Beauty—for something that gives life a taste and makes it meaningful. However, he never manages to find it, so that the story of his life, its "narrative unity"— as Alasdair MacIntyre would call it[37]—can be fittingly summed up with the movie's final words: "Blah, blah,

[36] Cf. ibid.: "These findings are consistent with the notion that premarital sex and cohabitation have become part of the normal courtship pattern in the United States. They do not indicate selectivity on characteristics linked to the risk of divorce and do not provide couples with experiences that lessen the stability of marriage."

[37] Cf. Alasdair MacIntyre, *After Virtue: A Study in Moral Theory*, 2nd ed. (Notre Dame: University of Notre Dame Press, 1984); see esp. chap. 15, "The Virtues, the Unity of a Human Life and the Concept of a Tradition" (pp. 204–25).

blah." All there is, is mere narrative fragmentation. And yet, on closer inspection, one can see that Jep Gambardella's main problem was not his inability to find the Great Beauty. His main problem was that he had found it—in the first woman he had ever loved, and with whom he had also had his first sexual experience—and then lost it. His entire life was to be marked by this loss. Every other relationship thereafter became trivial. The loss of the Great Beauty had bereft him of any authentic purpose in life, rich and respected though he was. Under this interpretation one could say that—perhaps ironically since it was probably unintended—the basic message of the film that deals a lot with superficial sexual encounters is precisely this: there is no casual sex.

It is common wisdom that it is much more expedient to preserve what is still intact than to fix what is broken. For this reason, remote marriage preparation is of extreme importance, and it may be a good idea to start it at an age *before* young people in a given society tend to become sexually active, which in the West would mean before their teenage years. They should be taught the meaning of human sexuality, namely, that it is for conjugal love. In this way, they will also quite naturally understand the meaning of premarital abstinence. It is evident that the Church is called to bind wounds and heal, but, as any medical doctor knows, the best medicine is prevention: to avoid people getting hurt in the first place. Young people are much more open to hearing about the virtue of chastity than is often assumed. Chastity talks, organized by the Student Life Office of the university I myself attended as a student, were usually among the best-attended extracurricular programs that were offered. There was hardly another topic all of us students were more desirous to learn about than the question of the true meaning of human sexuality. Chastity does not mean repressing the sexual urge but opening up a horizon of meaning in the context of which the sexual urge can be integrated. It is precisely because the exercise of our sexuality is for conjugal love, that is, because it implicates a life vocation, that chastity is not repressive but beautiful. Abstinence is not at all a negative repression of "evil" sex. It is not abstinence *from* but abstinence *for*: for one's future spouse, for whom it is beautiful, attractive, and meaningful to keep oneself, for him with whom one wants to build a common life. Any other perspective on human sexuality cheapens it and leaves the moral subject wounded and fragmented.

But people may say, "How to build a common life in the face of fate? How can I promise my life, if I don't know what the future holds?" It is true; very often things happen in life that are completely out of our power: illness, economic difficulties, problems with the children. In this situation—called the general human condition—how is it possible to promise one's life, including also what one will want in the future, and not just the authenticity of one's emotions, including only what one feels at the present? Here Robert Spaemann offers us a profound reflection when he suggests that by exchanging the marital vows, the spouses do not simply commit to hang on to their promise with an iron will, even if they should come to feel differently, even if they should come to regret their choice and change their minds.[38] Rather, the marital promise implies

---

[38] Robert Spaemann, *Persons: The Difference between "Someone" and "Something"*, trans. Oliver O'Donovan (Oxford: Oxford University Press, 2006), pp. 226–27: "Marriage is no ordinary promise to perform something, which

the promise to do everything in one's power to prevent coming into situations that would incline one to reconsider one's commitment to the other. While our feelings are not under our immediate control, our day-to-day decisions are. It is by the big and small choices we make every day that each of us develops our character and personality. We are constantly changing, and our choices are a major factor in this process. According to Spaemann, then, the marital vow is the promise "not to view the growth of one's personality as an independent variable that may or may not turn out to be compatible in some degree with the growth of the other's personality."[39] Thus the question, "What effect will such and such a choice have on the relationship with my spouse?" will become the decisive criterion for any decision that a married person will have to make. By assuming the married state, a person freely renounces the privilege of making choices solely on the basis of personal preference. If, as a single person, I live in Rome and get a job offer in the United States, the only question I need to ask is whether I'd like the job or not. If I'm married, I will also need to ask my wife if she wants to move with me, and if not, what it would mean for our relationship to leave her in another country and come home to her just once a month. These are the kind of choices that are entirely entrusted to our freedom and that make our marriages work out or fail.

---

one can still go through with when one has no mind to, or no longer feels the special interest that inclined one to the promise in the first place. With the marriage vow two people tie their fortunes together irrevocably—or that, at any rate, is what the vow intends. This promise could hardly be kept if one were in fact to change one's mind fundamentally."

[39] Ibid., p. 227.

However, in the journey of a common life, there will always be some things that truly just happen, events that are completely unrelated to our prior choices and for which we carry no responsibility at all. But even here, a married couple is not entirely at the mercy of fate. While by definition we cannot choose what merely happens, we can always choose how to respond to it. As Spaemann writes, "Marriage is predicated on the capacity of persons to create a structure for their life that is independent of unforeseen occurrences, delivering themselves from the control of chance by deciding once and for all in advance how such occurrences will be dealt with."[40] Being married means that some options one would otherwise have to react to a blow of fate are closed, given that marriage is a "lifelong sharing of destinies".[41] No longer having all the theoretical options open does not mean that one is no longer free. It just means that one's range of options has become delimited.[42] One could not possibly have actualized all the options anyway. Here the married person is not in any situation that is qualitatively different from the general human predicament: the moment we walk through one door, we close all the others. As Maurice Blondel convincingly points out, "We do not go forward, we do not learn, we do not enrich ourselves except by closing

[40] Ibid., p. 228.

[41] Ibid.

[42] Cf. ibid., p. 227: "At every stage of one's growth one is aware of the meaning it has for the other and for the other's growth. This is a very considerable restriction of our room to manoeuvre, but it is not a restriction of our *freedom*. For we could not in any case exhaust the whole range of possibilities. With every possibility we choose, we cancel others. If we do not wish to pay that price, we can never grasp the possibilities we have, and so never actually realize freedom."

off for ourselves all roads but one and by impoverishing ourselves of all that we might have known or gained otherwise.... I must commit myself under the pain of losing everything."[43] Freedom is given to be given, and only by being given is it actualized. By wanting to keep open all the options, we do not choose anything. But soon enough all the options we had or thought we had will close themselves off just by themselves.

4.5. The Path of Repentance

The same moral subject that finds it difficult to promise, binding himself for the future, also finds it difficult to repent and to ask for forgiveness, or to grant forgiveness, relating himself to the past. This brings us to the second solution Cardinal Kasper proposes to the problem of the divorced and civilly remarried. The Cardinal points out how "the Congregation for the Doctrine of the Faith provided a guideline already in 1994 when it declared—and Benedict XVI reiterated it at the World Meeting of Families in Milan in 2012—that the divorced and remarried admittedly cannot receive sacramental communion, but can indeed receive spiritual communion."[44] But if someone can be united to Christ spiritually, "why, then, can't he or she also receive sacramental communion?"[45] To the Cardinal's mind, the Church's practice of excluding from

---

[43] Maurice Blondel, *Action (1893): Essay on a Critique of Life and a Science of Practice*, trans. Oliva Blanchette (Notre Dame: University of Notre Dame Press, 2003), p. 4.

[44] *Gospel of the Family*, p. 30.

[45] Ibid.

sacramental Communion the divorced and remarried and of referring them to what he calls an "extrasacramental way of salvation" might "place the fundamental sacramental structure of the Church in question".[46]

At first sight, this reasoning may appear well-nigh impeccable. But then, again, it may all depend on what exactly we mean by "spiritual communion" and how we understand its relation to "sacramental communion". As Benoît-Dominique de La Soujeole points out, the expression has been used to refer to two different realities.[47] In the more original sense, the expression "spiritual communion" was used by Christian writers and Church documents to refer to the *fruit* of sacramental Communion, the state of being spiritually and most intimately united to Christ. In this sense, "sacramental communion is ordered to spiritual communion as the imperfect is to the perfect."[48] This is the sense implied by the Council of Trent when it distinguishes three ways of receiving the Eucharist: "some receive it *only sacramentally* because they are as sinners".[49] Then there are some "who receive it only *spiritually*; they are the ones who, receiving in desire the heavenly bread put before them, with a living faith 'working through love' [Gal 5:6], experience its fruit and benefit from it. The third group receive it both sacramentally and spiritually [*can. 8*];

[46] Ibid.

[47] Benoît-Dominique de La Soujeole, "Communion sacramentelle et communion spirituelle", *Nova et Vetera* 86, no. 2 (2011): 147–53.

[48] Quoted in ibid., p. 149: "La communion sacramentelle est ordonnée à la communion spirituelle comme l'imparfait l'est au parfait" (all translations by de La Soujeole are our own).

[49] The Council of Trent, Session 13, chapter 8, quoted in the English translation from *Henrich-Denzinger-Peter Hünermann, Compendium of Creeds, Definitions and Declarations on Matters of Faith and Morals* (San Francisco: Ignatius Press, 2012), p. 396, n. 1648.

they are the ones who examine and prepare themselves beforehand to approach this divine table, clothed in the wedding garment [*cf. Mt 22:11f.*]".[50]

When the Council speaks of those who receive Communion spiritually, it is not referring to those who abstain from sacramental Communion because they are aware of grave unconfessed sin or because they are publicly living in irregular life situations. Indeed, the Council Fathers speak of people with "a living faith 'working through love'", which is another way of saying that they are living in a state of grace. There may be various reasons for wanting to receive Communion by desire alone. For one, there is the cultural context of mediaeval and early modern times when many thought that by refraining from receiving Communion sacramentally, they would express a particular respect for the sacrament.[51] While today's understanding of how to honor the sacrament tends to be different, since frequent sacramental Communion is generally encouraged, we can still think of various nonmoral reasons for why persons would want to receive Communion by desire alone: they may want to honor the Eucharistic fast; they have arrived at Mass so late that they feel they are lacking the proper composure; they spontaneously and without actually sinning feel angry at another person who has wronged them just five minutes before Mass. According to de La Soujeole, we should think of a person receiving spiritual communion thus understood as someone who is "a fervent baptized person whose life receives its rhythm from the participation in the Eucharistic mystery, who

---

[50] Ibid.
[51] Cf. de La Soujeole, "Communion sacramentelle", p. 148, n. 5.

performs spiritual communions (acts of faith) in his daily life, and who in this way attains to the perfect fruit of the sacramental communion he has previously received".[52] If we understand "spiritual communion" in this way, Cardinal Kasper's objection follows with necessity: "The one who receives spiritual communion is one with Jesus Christ. How can he or she then be in contradiction to Christ's commandment? Why then, can't he or she also receive sacramental communion?"[53]

It seems, however, that recent Magisterial documents speak of "spiritual communion" in a different sense. In *Sacramentum caritatis* we read: "Even in cases where it is not possible to receive sacramental communion, participation at Mass remains necessary, important, meaningful and fruitful. In such circumstances it is beneficial to cultivate a desire for full union with Christ through the practice of spiritual communion, praised by Pope John Paul II and recommended by saints who were masters of the spiritual life" (no. 55). Here, the practice of spiritual Communion would not seem to refer to the fulfillment or fruit of sacramental Communion, but rather to "the desire of the Eucharistic sacrament".[54] While in the previous context "spiritual communion" referred to a true union of desire, here what seems to be at stake is only the desire of a union.[55] It is a desire that "as it grows can in

[52] Ibid., p. 151: "Il y a d'abord le cas du baptisé fervent dont la vie est comme 'rythmée' par la participation au mystère eucharistique, qui dans son existence quotidienne fait des communions spirituelles (actes de foi vive), qui atteint par là le fruit parfait de la communion sacramentelle qu'il ha reçu précédemment."

[53] *Gospel of the Family*, p. 30.

[54] Cf. de La Soujeole, "Communion sacramentelle", p. 150: "L'expression 'communion spirituelle' signifie ici le désir du sacrement eucharistique."

[55] Cf. ibid.

the end lead the sinner to break with the cause that still separates him from the sacrament and thus from the perfect spiritual communion with Christ, which is the fruit of the sacrament".[56] Spiritual communion is thus never "extrasacramental": it is always ordered to the sacrament. Indeed, in the present case it means cultivating one's desire for receiving Communion sacramentally.

This kind of spiritual communion concerns two categories of people. For one, there is the case of those who in their own consciences are aware of unconfessed grave sin. Spiritual communion, that is, the nurturing of the desire for the sacrament, will help them to open up to the grace of conversion, to receive the strength to turn away from their sin and avail themselves of the sacrament of reconciliation. But then "there is also the case of persons who, whatever the judgment of their conscience, are in an external situation that objectively contradicts Christian morality."[57] This is, for instance, the case of the divorced and civilly remarried. Here Cardinal Caffarra emphasizes that "the reason why the Church doesn't allow the divorced and remarried to receive Communion is not because she automatically presumes that they are all in a state of mortal sin. The Lord, who knows the heart, knows the subjective consciences of these people. St. Paul himself says 'do not judge rashly' but because, and this is written in *Familiaris Consortio*, 'their state and condition of life objectively contradict that union of love between Christ and

[56]Ibid.: "C'est ce désir qui, grandissant, peut à terme conduire le pécheur à rompre avec la cause qui le sépare encore du sacrement et donc de la communion spirituelle parfait avec le Christ qui est le fruit du sacrement."

[57]Ibid., p. 151: "C'est aussi le cas des personnes qui, quel que soit le jugement de leur conscience, sont dans une situation extérieure qui contredit objectivement la moral chrétienne."

the Church which is signified and effected by the Eucharist' (FC 84)."[58] Also Saint John Paul II observes that "the judgment of one's state of grace obviously belongs only to the person involved."[59] Each person is called to examine his own conscience and ultimately stand before God as his final judge. However, the Church does feel competent to judge a person's objective state of life, so that "in cases of outward conduct which is seriously, clearly and steadfastly contrary to the moral norm, the Church, in her pastoral concern for the good order of the community and out of respect for the sacrament, cannot fail to feel directly involved", in not admitting people who are living in such situations to Eucharistic Communion.[60]

Here, of course, Cardinal Kasper observes that "there are not *the* divorced and remarried."[61] In other words, given that each person's life situation is entirely particular, it is not possible to speak of objective life conditions. There are only individual cases, each of which has to be examined separately.[62] This, however, is said very nominalistically. In the same sense, then, there would not be *the* sinners, *the* righteous, *the* murderers, *the* thieves, or *the* virtuous, and yet sin, justice, murder, theft, and virtue are not empty concepts. If the acts that define a certain life situation can be objectively defined, then the life situation can also be

---

[58] Carlo Caffarra, "Da Bologna con amore: fermatevi", *Il Foglio*, March 14, 2014; English translation available at http://www.zenit.org/en/articles/cardinal-caffarra-expresses-serious-concerns-about-family-synod-debates#.

[59] John Paul II, Encyclical Letter *Ecclesia de Eucharistia*, April 17, 2003, no. 37.
[60] Ibid.
[61] *Gospel of the Family*, p. 45; emphasis in original.
[62] Cardinal Kasper also observes that "there also is not *the* objective situation, which poses an obstacle to admission to communion, but rather many very different objective situations" (ibid.).

objectively defined, without having to take recourse to circumstances or intentions. *That* acts can be thus defined is the explicit teaching of John Paul II's encyclical *Veritatis splendor:* "Without in the least denying the influence on morality exercised by circumstances and especially by intentions, the Church teaches that 'there exist acts which *per se* and in themselves, independently of circumstances, are always seriously wrong by reason of their object.' "[63] It is true that why and how people get into the situation of being divorced and remarried is always different and particular, and it is true that the intentions and circumstances can be alleviating or aggravating, but never justifying. Given that their objective situation is defined by particular, clearly describable acts, this situation is not only similar but the *same:* it is a condition in which two live together and habitually perform acts proper to spouses, even though they are not married,[64] and at least one of them is married to someone else.

Thus, when the Church is judging that a given state of life is contrary to the teaching of the Gospel, there is actually something she can judge. When she does not admit to Communion those who find themselves in such a situation, she does not mete out a punishment. Rather, she invites them to change their state of life (to separate or to live as brother and sister). This invitation takes them seriously as persons, that is, as individuals whose lives are not something that simply happens to them, but who are able to *lead* their lives because they *possess* their lives and who, by the

[63] *VS* 80.

[64] As we have argued at length, according to the teaching of the Church, the civil recognition of their union does not change the fact that they are *not* married.

grace of God, are able to change their objective conditions. In fact, the Church is acting here as any loving mother would with respect to her children. Love accepts the other unconditionally—the Church encourages spiritual communion and emphasizes that the divorced and remarried are part of her—and yet love at the same time does everything to call the other on, to make him grow, even to encourage the beloved to change radically if he lives in a way that hurts the family's communion and contradicts his own good. This is what the Church does by not admitting the divorced and civilly remarried to sacramental Communion; she loves them by inviting them to change. She does not deny the medicine of the Eucharist to someone who "cries for help", instrumentalizing a person by making "him or her into a sign for others". Nor does she let "him or her starve sacramentally so that others may live".[65] Not every food is good for everyone (cf. 1 Cor 3:2), and not every medicine is healing in every condition. There are medicines that, if wrongly applied, can kill.

Cardinal Kasper rightly refers to the surpassing generosity and grace our Lord lavishes on the repentant sinner: "For the one who repents, forgiveness is possible. If forgiveness is possible for the murderer, then it is also possible for the adulterer."[66] There is no doubt about this. In his interview to *Die Tagespost*, Prof. Juan José Pérez-Soba warned against developments that could make adultery the first sin for which it is possible to receive forgiveness without repenting.[67] Cardinal Kasper, in turn, granting an interview to the Catholic news website Kath.net, responded

---

[65] *Gospel of the Family*, p. 30.

[66] Ibid., p. 32.

[67] Juan José Pérez-Soba, "Tiefgründigster Interpret des Konzils", *Die Tagespost*, March 13, 2014, p. 5: "Die Barmherzigkeit klopft an der Tür des

that he did indeed speak about the need of repentance and that the whole issue was a "phantom discussion" in which he was criticized for positions he never actually held.[68] To learn that a simple misunderstanding was at the bottom of the debate would be most welcome. To find out whether this is the case, we will take another look at what Cardinal Kasper is saying in *The Gospel of the Family* about the need for repentance on the part of the divorced and remarried:

> But if a divorced and remarried person is truly sorry that he or she failed in the first marriage, if the commitments from the first marriage are clarified and a return is definitively

---

Geschiedenen, damit dieser dem sakramentalen Ehebund treu bleibt und sich nie außerhalb stellt. Würde Barmherzigkeit etwas anderes bedeuten dann wäre Ehebruch—denn so nennt Jesus selbst eine neue Verbindung—die einzige Sünde, die ohne Reue vergeben werden könnte." (Mercy knocks at the door of the divorced so that he or she may remain faithful to the sacramental marriage bond and never place himself or herself outside of it. If mercy were to mean something different, then adultery—for this is how Jesus himself calls a new union—would be the only sin that can be forgiven without repentance); translation our own.

[68] "Kasper: 'Für eine bloße Phantomdiskussion ist das Problem zu ernst!'", April 22, 2014, http://www.kath.net/news/45617: "Es geht im Vortrag nicht mehr um die Zulassung zur Kommunion, sondern um die Zulassung zum Sakrament der Buße und damit zur Absolution. Die Buße setzt voraus, dass Schuld gegeben und bereut wird, aber ebenso dass Gott dem, der umkehrt, barmherzig ist und die Schuld vergibt. Die Behauptung, ich betrachte den Ehebruch als die einzige Sünde, die ohne Reue vergeben werde, ist barer Unsinn, wie es Unsinn ist, Barmherzigkeit werde von mir als Toleranz des Bösen verstanden.... [W]er sich mit meinen Fragen auseinandersetzen will, sollte kritisieren, was wirklich dasteht. Für eine bloße Phantomdiskussion ist das Problem zu ernst!" (The topic of the presentation was no longer the admittance to Communion but the admittance to the sacrament of penance and thus to absolution. Repentance presupposes that there is guilt and that the guilt is repented of. At the same time, it presupposes that God is merciful to everyone who converts, forgiving his or her guilt. The claim that I consider adultery the only sin that can be forgiven without repentance is sheer nonsense, just as it is nonsense that I understand mercy as the tolerance of evil.... Whoever wishes to engage my questions should criticize what is written in the book. The problem is too serious for a mere phantom discussion!); translation our own.

out of the question, if he or she cannot undo the commitments that were assumed in the second civil marriage
without new guilt, if he or she strives to the best of his or
her abilities to live out the second civil marriage on the
basis of faith and to raise their children in the faith, if he
or she longs for the sacraments as a source of strength in
his or her situation, do we then have to refuse or can we
refuse him or her the sacrament of penance and communion, after a period of reorientation?[69]

The author is of course introducing the topic of repentance here, when he says, "If a divorced and remarried
person is truly sorry ..." But what follows then is among
the most peculiar details of the whole booklet. What is the
divorced and remarried sorry for? Is he sorry for having
violated the marital covenant with his spouse, a covenant
that is a sacramental sign of God's love for his Church? Is
he sorry for having committed adultery by having sexual
relations with a person to whom he is not married?[70] No,
for all this the divorced and remarried person is not "truly
sorry" but rather for the fact "that he or she failed in the
first marriage".[71]

Now we can only promise what is in our power to
do or not do. The marital promise cannot be a promise
that one's marriage will succeed, since success or failure
in a marriage does not depend on the individual alone. It
takes two to tango, and at times there may even be circumstances outside the power of both that may strongly

[69] *Gospel of the Family*, p. 32.
[70] After all, a valid and consummated sacramental marriage is indissoluble.
Cf. ibid., p. 43: "No one questions the indissolubility of a sacramental marriage
that was contracted and consummated (*ratum* and *consumatum*)."
[71] Ibid., p. 32.

contribute to marital failure, making it difficult to pass the blame. In another scenario, the guilt for the failure may just be with one, in which case there is another who is without fault. A marital failure, which may lead to separation, is not yet a breaking of the marital promises, and as such not in itself something of which one necessarily needs to repent. One may have to repent of freely chosen acts that have led up to it, but then again, one may also have done everything in one's power to prevent it.

If on the day of their wedding the bride and groom do not promise each other marital success, what do they promise each other? They promise each other exclusivity and faithfulness unto death. This promise can be maintained even if under some circumstances it will become intolerable to continue living together. Only if the spouses take this promise seriously will they invest every effort into their relationship; only then will they resist the temptation to consider themselves campers who simply move on if they feel inconvenienced. Each will be the one and only chance for the other. "You are my one and only", the lover says to the beloved. "Even in the now unimaginable case that our love should fail, you will still be my one and only. I will always leave a light on for you." Indissolubility of marriage means that the door remains always open for the other, even in the case of separation from bed and roof. The marital promise is only broken once a new union is sought. Whether this new union is now approved by the State or not makes much less difference than the Cardinal suggests. It is true that *Familiaris consortio* admonishes pastors of souls to distinguish carefully "between those who have sincerely tried to save their first marriage and have been unjustly abandoned and those who, through their

own grave fault, have destroyed a canonically valid marriage" and to be aware of the subjective situation of those
"who have entered into a second union for the sake of
the children's upbringing and who are sometimes subjectively certain in conscience that their previous irreparably
destroyed marriage had never been valid"[72]. It is also correct that John Paul II's exhortation does not use the term
"adulterous union". The same document, however, also
makes it clear that nonetheless in *all* these cases we are
dealing with a way of life that is "in contradiction to the
indissolubility of marriage".[73]

According to *Familiaris consortio*, what needs repentance is not the failure of the first marriage but the fact of
"having broken the sign of the covenant and of fidelity to
Christ".[74] The first thing repentance implies is a change
in one's behavior. In this case it implies the readiness "to
undertake a way of life that is no longer in contradiction
to the indissolubility of marriage".[75] Cardinal Kasper rightly
argues that "if forgiveness is possible for the murderer,
then it is also possible for the adulterer."[76] And yet, to
be forgiven, the murderer has to repent. The first sign of
repentance for him is to stop murdering. Cardinal Kasper
speaks about "the path of permitting divorced people, who
are civilly remarried, to receive the sacrament of penance
and the Eucharist in concrete situations, after a period of
reorientation".[77] Here I'm not sure that I'm able to see a

[72] *FC* 84.
[73] Ibid.
[74] Ibid.
[75] Ibid.
[76] *Gospel of the Family*, p. 32.
[77] Ibid., p. 52.

path. With all due respect—and always allowing for the possibility that there is a misunderstanding—to my mind the image that suggests itself here is not so much that of a path than that of a treadmill. The divorced and remarried seem to be invited to walk (they do acts of penance) without going anywhere (they continue to share the same roof and the same bed).

If a man came to a priest to receive the sacrament of reconciliation, confessing that he had stolen his neighbor's Ferrari, what will the priest tell him? To do penance? Yes. To make a pilgrimage, recite some extra prayers, and give alms? Perhaps. Before all else, however, one would suppose the priest to exhort him to return the car and to make the penitent's firm will of doing so a condition for absolution. It is hardly thinkable that a pastor of souls would advise his penitent that after a year of penance he can officially start using the vehicle, as long as there are no legal consequences to be feared. I am rather certain that Cardinal Kasper would insist that the case he is making for admitting some of the divorced and remarried to the sacraments is different, and I am more than open to learning how it would be so in the relevant aspects.

Indeed, the Cardinal emphasizes that the *oikonomia* which he proposes "is not a cheap path or an expedient escape. It takes seriously that, as Martin Luther formulated it correctly in the first of his Ninety-Five Theses in 1517, the entire Christian life is one of penance, that is, a life of repeatedly new rethinking and reorientation (*metanoia*)."[78] It is precisely this rethinking and reorientation that according to *Familiaris consortio* is still too imperfect in the

[78] Ibid., p. 51.

divorced and civilly remarried who insist on having continued intimate relations outside their one true sacramental marriage.[79] While the Reformer was able to suggest that no sin can separate us from the Lamb, "even if we fornicated or killed a thousand times a day",[80] the authority of our Lord Jesus himself would seem to be greater: "Neither do I condemn you; go, and do not sin again" (Jn 8:11).

---

[79] FC 84.

[80] Martin Luther, Letter to Philipp Melanchthon, no. 424, August 1, 1521, in *Werke. Kritische Gesamtausgabe. Briefwechsel. 2. Band* (Weimar: Hermann Böhlaus Nachfolger, 1931), p. 372: "Sufficit, quod agnovimus per divitias gloriae Dei agnum, qui tollit peccatum mundi; ab hoc non avellet nos peccatum, etiamsi millies, millies uno die fornicemur aut occidamus." (Let it be enough that through the riches of the glory of God we have known the Lamb who takes away the sin of the world; no sin will separate us from him, even if we fornicated or killed a thousand times a day); translation our own.

5

A Pastoral Ministry of Mercy:
Living the Truth in Charity

"Today, the theological and canonical debate seems rarefied. Generally speaking, the number of formally established marriages has diminished; so has the number of sacramental marriages. Those in the typical situation of the pastoral problem of divorced-and-remarried Catholics ... seem to accept more and more the forms of structured welcome that the Church throughout the world is organizing and conducting."[1] This description of the situation is the work of one of the authors most in favor of offering Holy Communion to the divorced and remarried, on one simple condition: that the previous marriage be declared irremediably failed. He observes, moreover, that this is a less urgent pastoral issue than several years ago, and that the change in trend that emerges from a series of sociological studies shows the extent of cohabitation without any type of bond.[2] It is increasingly obvious that divorced

[1] Basilio Petrà, *Divorziati risposati e seconde nozze nella Chiesa: Una via di soluzione* (Assisi: Cittadella, 2012), p. 38.

[2] See the Eleventh Report on the Family in Italy (*XI Rapporto Famiglia CISF*), which also presents a series of statistics on the European situation: Pierpaolo Donati, ed., *La relazione di coppia oggi: Una sfida per la famiglia* (Trento: Erickson, 2012).

people *do not remarry*. The more serious pastoral problem is therefore quite different and is reflected in the evident decrease in the percentage of the population that is married in the Western world.[3]

Consequently, in the present situation it does not seem appropriate, much less prudent, to focus on the issue of the divorced and remarried, since that does not spring from an authentic pastoral vision. The problems of the family are manifold and diverse; an awareness of the necessity to be close to those in need so as to offer them effective help prompts us to adopt a pastoral approach of "accompaniment". Unfortunately, though, we must point out that the current pastoral structures in most parts of the Church are based more on organizing activities or dictating pastoral norms than on accompanying persons. The pastoral effort required of us today by the reality of families is greater than the effort that might be demanded by one specific problem, and it is connected with the profound mercy that Christ holds in his heart. The lack of this universal pastoral vision is the greatest defect in Cardinal Kasper's address. The Cardinal mentions several obvious questions without proposing *anything* on this subject, as though it were of little importance or, at least, not worth mentioning.[4] What he acknowledges is undeniable:

[3] Cf. Irène Théry, *Le démariage: Justice et vie privée* (Paris: Odile Jacob, 1993).

[4] These matters are mentioned a few times but without any in-depth examination; the introduction presents a long series of problems, but once they are listed, they are not discussed: "Many families today see that they are confronted with serious *difficulties*. Many millions of people find themselves in situations of migration, flight, and forced displacement, or in degrading situations of misery, in which an orderly family life is scarcely possible. The contemporary world finds itself in an *anthropological crisis*. Individualism and consumerism challenge the traditional culture of families. *Economic conditions* often make family cohesion and living together more difficult. Consequently, the number of those

One may not reduce the problem *to the question of admission to communion*. It touches upon *pastoral care for marriage and family life in their totality*. It begins already with pastoral care for youth and with *marriage preparation*, which should be a thorough catechesis for marriage and family life. The task continues with the *pastoral accompaniment* of married couples and families. It becomes relevant and immediate when a marriage or a family is plunged into a crisis. In this situation, pastoral ministers will do everything possible to contribute to *healing and reconciling* the marriage and the family that has fallen into crisis.[5]

In the Italian edition, Cardinal Kasper's text continues: "Pastoral care does not end after the failure of a marriage; pastors must *stay close to the divorced* and invite them to participate in the life of the Church."[6] In reality, though, these are broad, vague observations that can be made without any pastoral concern for understanding their significance within the Church's program of action. Little attention is paid to these topics, which are a long way from being included in the Church's present concerns. And that only makes sense, if we realize that he presents any other

---

who back away from establishing a family or who fail to realize their life's goal, as well as the number of children who do not have the good fortune of growing up in a well-ordered family, has increased dramatically" (*Gospel of the Family*, pp. 1–2; emphasis added).

It should be noted, however, that another presentation of the question, this time from the perspective of the divorced and remarried, appears in ibid., p. 25, and in the final conclusion (p. 33), in which the author acknowledges that there are "other difficult pastoral situations that have not been mentioned in this context".

[5] Ibid., pp. 25–26; emphasis added.

[6] Cf. Walter Kasper, *Il vangelo della famiglia* (Brescia: Queriniana, 2014), p. 42. For some reason this phrase does not appear in the German version, on which the English translation seems to be based.

topic as hinging *exclusively* on the divorced. The address is not aimed at accompanying *all* families within the scope of pastoral ministry for holiness; in other words, it does not lead concretely to an authentic evangelization of the family.

It is true that earlier the Cardinal presented a beautiful description of the family as the domestic church, pointing out its centrality as the subject of evangelization and recalling the many resources that it has for bringing the Gospel to life.[7] In this exhortation, however, the family is presented as already established, and at no point is any indication given concerning the pastoral response that this involves; everything remains immersed in a sort of spontaneous family life, without realizing concretely that in this development the family needs very definite help from the Church. In other words, the ideal role of families is perfectly well acknowledged, but from the perspective of a distant observer, who offers nothing but fine words. Families are not considered as the central pillar of pastoral care, with all that this involves at the ecclesial level. This respectful reference will help him, actually, to turn to a general exhortation about the family in his fine conclusion.[8]

---

[7] See the section on "The Family as Domestic Church" in ibid., pp. 20–25, in which he declares, "[Families] are not only the *object*, but also the *subject* of family pastoral care" (p. 23). On this topic cf. Giacomo Verrengia, *La famiglia, soggetto attivo e responsabile nell'evangelizzazione* (Naples: Laurenziana, 1996).

[8] This could be summed up in the following statement: "In families, the Church encounters the reality of life. Therefore, families are the test case for pastoral care and the most serious test case for the new evangelization" (*Gospel of the Family*, p. 34). Concerning this subject as the principle of organic pastoral ministry, see Claudio Giuliodori, "La famiglia cristiana, protagonista della nuova evangelizzazione", in Juan José Pérez-Soba, ed., *La famiglia, luce di Dio in una società senza Dio: Nuova evangelizzazione e famiglia* (Siena: Cantagalli, 2014), pp. 87–110.

Therefore, from the outset, we can say that Kasper's address is short on pastoral inspiration and long on normative and doctrinal interest, contrary to his own claims. He ends by speaking about the gospel of the family, but without giving any indication of how to design organic, incisive pastoral care that truly evangelizes. This should not surprise us, given the marginal position of the family in the Church's pastoral ministry—so much so that many pastors, despite their good intentions, really do not know what to do. This is precisely what is supposed to be remedied in the upcoming Synods. Naturally, the pastoral approach of *Familiaris consortio* offers a broader vision, which in many respects is yet to be implemented; it has proved to be very fruitful[9] in places where it has been put into practice.[10]

5.1. Pastoral Ministry of Mercy

No doubt, any pastoral activity is rooted in the mercy of the heart of Christ. The Gospel account is extremely eloquent: "When he saw the crowds, he had compassion for them, because they were harassed and helpless, like sheep without a shepherd" (Mt 9:36). The compassion of the heart of Christ is the source of his care for individuals, which begins with his choice of the Twelve immediately afterward (see Mt 10:1). The Lord's activity, which comes from the heart, is connected with serious human failings, but above all with the grandeur of the divine plan, since

[9] See the essays in Livio Melina, ed., "Il futuro di una via: la fecondità di *Familiaris consortio* 30 anni dopo", in *Anthropotes* 28, no. 1 (2012).

[10] See the wealth of pastoral testimonies in Livio Melina, ed., *Giovanni Paolo II, il Papa della Famiglia* (Rome: Cantagalli, 2014).

what he does right away is "to teach them many things" (Mk 6:34). Human miseries are the motive for his attention, but the purpose of Christ's activity is union with God for a people that demonstrates that the Kingdom of God is real in the midst of mankind.[11]

In order to be able to understand the fundamental character of the *pastoral perspective*, it is important to enter into the unique glance of the heart of Christ, as the "heart which sees".[12] This involves being particularly sensitive to what God is asking in each situation: it is an affective perspective that starts from the *concrete situation*. The truth of love that guides it has an exceptional characteristic: an amazing universality, since love extends to all human beings, and a lofty concreteness that appreciates every circumstance and human event.[13] That is why pastoral ministry must follow this logic of love,[14] which is quite different from the technical logic of problem solving. This is something apparently very simple, but unfortunately it is an attitude that seems to have been adopted in our pastoral structures rarely, if at all. The change that is required of us here will be very profound, and it will take a lot of time to adopt it in a relevant way in our Church.

[11] See *EG* III: "[The Church] is certainly a *mystery* rooted in the Trinity, yet she exists concretely in history as a people of pilgrims and evangelizers" (emphasis added).

[12] See *DCE* 31 b: "The Christian's programme—the programme of the Good Samaritan, the programme of Jesus—is 'a heart which sees'. This heart sees where love is needed and acts accordingly. Obviously when charitable activity is carried out by the Church as a communitarian initiative, the spontaneity of individuals must be combined with planning, foresight and cooperation with other similar institutions."

[13] On this issue, cf. Juan José Pérez-Soba, *La verità dell'amore: Una luce per camminare: Esperienza, metafisica e fondamento della morale* (Siena: Cantagalli, 2011).

[14] See *LG* 27.

This, then, is what we can call a "pastoral ministry of mercy": a pastoral ministry that has its own specific content and contains its own truth. In this way we avoid any reduction of our approach to an ill-defined attitude, especially if there is a risk, as we said, of it being confused with mere tolerance or with a subjective movement of compassion toward the sufferings of others. As we said about mercy, it is not a question of seeking tolerance with respect to a problem, but rather of being much more aware of the regenerating role of grace in the life of individual persons, without denying the profound change of life that this presupposes.

In fact, the perspective of mercy helps us to discover the decisive importance of the pastoral care of the family, since it directly involves the source of the greatest human sufferings. In the first place, this is because in our present-day culture, which is marked by a rampant individualism,[15] the greatest sickness is *loneliness*. This is a new and particularly bitter poverty, in which we hear an echo of the divine compassion: "It is not good that the man should be alone" (Gen 2:18). Whereas in the biblical account (in the same verse) God's response to this loneliness is the communion of the family, so that God gives the man "a helper fit for him", nowadays the preceding statement takes on a different and urgent meaning: "It is not good for the family to be alone."[16] Consequently, pastoral attention to the family is not just a strategic matter of defending an institution that is especially under attack, but rather it springs from a deeper realization of the role of the family within

[15] See *EG* 63.

[16] See José Granados, *Nessuna famiglia è un'isola: Le radici di una istituzione nella società e nella Chiesa* (Milan: Paoline, 2013).

the Church. It consists in understanding the divine design for the Christian family—a plan that contains within it the merciful heart of Christ. It is of fundamental importance to respond to this need in order to revitalize the Church in her evangelizing impetus. It is a matter of faith, because there is an obvious connection between the weakening of the faith and the crisis of the family institution,[17] as Pope Benedict XVI brought to light in the context of the preceding Synod:

> Marriage is linked to faith, but not in a general way. Marriage, as a union of faithful and indissoluble love, is based upon the grace that comes from the triune God, who in Christ loved us with a faithful love, even to the Cross. Today we ought to grasp the full truth of this statement, in contrast to the painful reality of many marriages which, unhappily, end badly. There is a clear link between the crisis in faith and the crisis in marriage.[18]

The upcoming Synods that will be held in October of 2014 and 2015 are designed to be pastoral and therefore are in keeping with the solicitude for the family that all the popes have shown, with particular intensity after the Second Vatican Council, which intended to underscore the fact that "the well-being of the individual person and of both

---

[17]See Giovanna Rossi, "Famiglia e trasmissione della fede", in Pérez-Soba, *Nuova evangelizzazione e famiglia*, pp. 35–75.

[18] "Holy Mass for the Opening of the Synod of Bishops and Proclamation of St. John of Avila and of St. Hildegard of Bingen as 'Doctors of the Church': Homily of His Holiness Pope Benedict XVI", October 7, 2012. This led him to conclude: "It [struck me] that the Synod repeatedly emphasized the significance, for the transmission of the faith, of the family as the authentic setting in which to hand on the blueprint of human existence" ("Address of His Holiness Benedict XVI on the Occasion of Christmas Greetings to the Roman Curia", December 21, 2012).

human and Christian society is closely bound up with the healthy state of conjugal and family life."[19] Consequently, the Council proposes the family as the first of the "more urgent problems deeply affecting the human race at the present day".[20] This is an extremely urgent appeal, since in fact we observe a discrepancy between a plain exhortation to be dedicated to the pastoral care of the family and the great poverty of the Church in this dimension.

5.2. To Generate Life: The Truth of a Love

To speak about the family means to speak about a kind of good news for mankind, about an authentic gospel in a well-defined pastoral sense.[21] This is more important than an interminable list of problems that we could easily draw up simply by observing what is happening around us; but this runs the risk of leading to a series of sterile lamentations instead of a true pastoral care in the proper sense. Once again, Jesus Christ is instructive with his heart of a Good Shepherd. Certainly, he is perfectly aware of these difficulties, but his glance goes *beyond*—his activity is defined not by the difficulties that must be overcome, but rather by the *mission that he is called to accomplish*: "I came that they may have life, and have it abundantly" (Jn 10:10).

One of the main points for appropriately orienting the pastoral care of the family is to get over the outmoded idea of pastoral care focused on problem solving, which has

[19] GS 47.

[20] GS 46.

[21] See Livio Melina, "Il Vangelo della famiglia, davanti a noi. Prefazione", in Livio Melina and José Granados, eds., *Famiglia e nuova evangelizzazione: la chiave dell'annuncio* (Siena: Cantagalli, 2012), pp. 5–15.

proved useless and, in many instances, even caused discouragement and produced a certain secularizing effect. When one's intention is focused exclusively on identifying solutions to problems, they usually multiply in an unexpected way, resulting in the impression of being overwhelmed by a reality that seems to have an origin completely different from the Gospel. This easily gives rise to the temptation simply to adapt to the demands of the present day, since that seems to be the only way to obtain some positive result from such an adverse situation. It is not difficult to recognize, in this scenario, a consequentialist mindset that distrusts the ability of the Gospel to renew persons and to change the tendencies of our culture. This could happen if the Synod gave in to pressure from some individuals and focused mainly on the problem of Communion for the divorced and remarried. In the attempt to identify, in one way or another, a satisfactory solution, one runs the risk of causing many new problems.

In the case of the family, this demand is particularly important, because it is a radical change of pastoral perspective. To proclaim the gospel of the family means to communicate life;[22] therefore it is necessary to employ those features that define the way in which this life is developed, and, in that sense, there can be no clearer path than mercy: "returning to life" (cf. Lk 15:32; Ezek 18:21–23). Now we can speak therefore comprehensively about *the truth of love* as the truth that constructs the authentic *identity of all persons*, based on a divine vocation and derived from a series of well-defined steps: "This itinerary, being a son, so

---

[22] See Juan José Pérez-Soba, *La pastorale familiare: tra programmazioni pastorali e generazione di una vita* (Siena: Cantagalli, 2013). Here the reader can find the arguments that justify the preceding statements.

as then to be a husband and eventually a father, expresses the set of basic human relationships that establish these personal—and not merely natural—bonds that frame the actions of human beings."[23]

Love has the ability to generate actions; it is not a mere application of norms, since there is always the originality and the specificity of the beloved in a personal history. This responds to a dynamic, operative truth, moved by the tension of unity in difference.[24] Clearly the law is not sufficient to determine a direct action based on the truth of love, but, at the same time, it is easy to understand that the law internally contains a "truth of the good" that has an objective character that must always be preserved. If I truly love a person, I do not want just any good for her, but the *true* good, the good of the person, by which the beloved becomes good as a person; otherwise I betray my love.[25] The truth of love is therefore a principle that serves to reinforce the conviction that there are intrinsically bad acts that can never be the expression of the charity of Christ, and that always must be regarded as the "death of love", as the loss of the relationship with God, who is Love: "He who does not love remains in death" (1 Jn 3:14).[26]

---

[23] Livio Melina, José Noriega, and Juan José Pérez-Soba, *Camminare nella luce dell'amore: I fondamenti della morale cristiana*, 2nd ed. (Siena: Cantagalli, 2010), p. 123.

[24] See Angelo Scola, *Identidad y diferencia* (Madrid: Encuentro, 1989). For the following discussion, cf. Livio Melina, *Azione epifania dell'amore: La morale cristiana oltre il moralismo e l'antimoralismo* (Siena: Cantagalli, 2008).

[25] Cf. on this point Livio Melina, " 'Verità sul bene': Razionalità pratica, etica filosofica e teologia morale: Da 'Veritatis splendor' a 'Fides et ratio'", *Anthropotes* 15 (1999): 125–43.

[26] See Saint Thomas Aquinas, *Duo praecepta caritatis*, Prol. III, no. 1140: "si quis habet omnia dona Spiritus sancti absque caritate, non habet vitam." (If someone has all the gifts of the Holy Spirit except charity, he has no life.)

It is altogether inadequate to design a pastoral program that does not take into account the moral truth of the action performed in light of the law, or that falls into the temptation to measure its actual expediency only by means of technical results, or else that confuses mercy, as we said, with compassion to the detriment of the truth of justice.

In our case, the reality of the indissolubility of marriage is a dimension of the revelation of a love that is freely given, in other words, of something that is not at the disposal of the person who receives it, but is a preceding truth illuminated by God. All we can do is live by our relationship with this gift. In the same way, someone who receives baptism, although he has received inadequate preparation and has no subsequent formation, nevertheless possesses a gift of God's salvation. Pastorally, this has always been interpreted as the need for ecclesial support so that the person might become aware of his baptismal consecration and of the necessity for subsequent catechesis along these lines.

Therefore the real extent of indissolubility ("what God has joined") is explained in terms of the revelation of the gift, not in terms of simple praxis, and this reveals at the same time the extent of the Church's responsibility with respect to this gift. To look for an exception to this quality of marriage is therefore not a pastoral criterion; the gift itself is what creates bonds of justice that must be honored. The discernment that it requires is quite different: how to make the gift that has been received grow in the consciences and in the lives of the faithful.

Pastorally, the gift of indissolubility, rather than a limit to be overcome, is a strength, an enormous resource that sustains every marriage, and any pastoral care must be founded upon it. This is the specific evangelizing perspective of the true pastoral care of the family, the *holiness of families*, something that can never be regarded as elitist[27] inasmuch as a holy family is one that discovers the marvelous mission of helping other families along this path. It is the principle of a surprising pastoral and evangelizing capability, the true apostolic path of the family within our society. Unfortunately, though, this is not how most people view the real role of the family in the life of the Church, which has been discouraged by a culture opposed to the family.[28]

5.3. The Truth of Pastoral Activity as an Evangelizing Act as Opposed to False Pastoral Solutions

From what we were able to read in Kasper's address, his insistence on mercy is aimed at making it an innovative principle of pastoral ministry. In fact, the Cardinal goes so far as to identify the two things, pastoral ministry and mercy, adopting this novel point of view: "Pastoral care and mercy are not contradictory to justice, but are, so to speak, the higher righteousness."[29] The statement alludes to the existence of a "pastoral reason" higher than justice that would somehow allow us to revise the latter.

But how? This is where the argument as a whole tends to identify both terms with a certain tolerance, among other things maintaining that "out of pastoral concern 'to prevent something worse,' these fathers were willing to tolerate

---

[27] This is alluded to in *Gospel of the Family*, p. 25, where the Cardinal cites *EG* 197–201.

[28] See Livio Melina, ed., *Il criterio della natura e il futuro della famiglia* (Siena: Cantagalli, 2011).

[29] *Gospel of the Family*, p. 29.

something that, in itself, is unacceptable."[30] This danger-ous statement seems to suggest the acceptance of something that, in itself, is unjust. This is essential to an understanding of the deeper reason for this proposal: the search for an exception to an ecclesial norm that is considered exces-sively severe. The argument is based therefore on the idea that there are possibilities that the norm, as such, does not contemplate. This way of presenting pastoral practice has already been used several times for the purpose of avoiding some moral requirements connected with the existence of intrinsically evil acts. As *Veritatis splendor* declares: "On this basis, an attempt is made to legitimize so-called 'pastoral' solutions contrary to the teaching of the Magisterium, and to justify a 'creative' hermeneutic according to which the moral conscience is in no way obliged, in every case, by a particular negative precept."[31]

John Paul II speaks about the real intention of an allegedly "higher pastoral reason" that some describe as "merciful" or "tolerant", which claims at least to excuse the failure to abide by some moral precepts. To accept this way of understanding benevolent pastoral care, as opposed to the "rigidity of the law", is clearly to run the risk of falling into a sort of subjectivism. Benedict XVI called attention to this point very forcefully: "One must avoid pseudo-pastoral claims that would situate questions on a purely horizontal plane, in which what matters is to satisfy subjective requests."[32]

[30] Ibid., p. 31. He continued, "There was, therefore, a pastoral practice of tolerance, clemency, and forbearance".

[31] *VS* 56.

[32] "Address of His Holiness Pope Benedict XVI on the Occasion of the Inauguration of the Judicial Year of the Tribunal of the Roman Rota", Jan-uary 29, 2010; his address deals with the relation between charity and justice.

The real criterion for acting pastorally is very different. The truth of the pastoral action must actualize the specific twofold level of the truth of love that was discussed earlier. On the one hand, it must maintain the *concrete and unique bond* with the beloved person, and, on the other hand, it must correspond to the *objective character of the good* inasmuch as "it is communicable in and of itself",[33] in other words, has a universal import.[34] As a personal act, love has a unique "creativity", which is essential as an element of "newness" in our world, with deep theological roots,[35] but it never goes against the moral truth of the action.

Reason distinguishes the value of negative precepts, which can *never* be transgressed, from positive norms, which are open to a higher measure:

> The commandment of love of God and neighbor does not have in its dynamic any higher limit, but it does have a lower limit, beneath which the commandment is broken. Furthermore, what must be done in any given situation depends on the circumstances, not all of which can be foreseen; on the other hand there are kinds of behavior which can never, in any situation, be a proper response—a response which is in conformity with the dignity of the person. Finally, it is always possible that man, as the result of coercion or other circumstances, can be hindered from

[33] See *EG* 9: "Goodness always tends to spread."

[34] See Livio Melina, "Acting for the Good of Communion", in *The Epiphany of Love. Toward a Theological Understanding of Christian Action* (Grand Rapids, Mich.: Eerdman, 2010), pp. 25–45.

[35] See José Granados, " 'Trajo toda la novedad, al traerse a sí mismo': apuntes para una teología de lo nuevo", in Juan José Pérez-Soba and Eleonora Stefanyan, eds., *L'azione, fonte di novità: Teoria dell'azione e compimento della persona: ermeneutiche a confronto* (Siena: Cantagalli, 2010), pp. 285–303.

doing certain good actions; but he can never be hindered
from not doing certain actions, especially if he is prepared
to die rather than to do evil.[36]

The reason is simple: one may *never* offend the dignity of
a human person. Absolute respect for the negative norm
is a necessary limit so as not to offend against this personal dignity that is at stake in human acts with respect
to certain goods: "These negative precepts express with
particular force the ever urgent need to protect human life,
the communion of persons in marriage, private property,
truthfulness and people's good name."[37]

Far from being a problem for pastoral ministry, the limit
set by the law with respect to these acts is the evangelizing
principle par excellence. The Church has always understood it as being joined with martyrdom, which shows
human dignity in the gift of one's life as a manifestation of
the greatness of the faith.[38] In the same way, we certainly
must recall the witness of faithful marriages, which testifies
before a skeptical world to the truth of a lasting love.[39]

What is at stake here is the "good of the person", which
must always be affirmed and defended—a good that goes

[36] *VS* 52. This is based on the Pope's statement that "the *negative precepts* of
the natural law are universally valid. They oblige each and every individual,
always and in every circumstance. It is a matter of prohibitions which forbid a
given action *semper et pro semper*, without exception, because the choice of this
kind of behavior is in no case compatible with the goodness of the will of the
acting person, with his vocation to life with God and to communion with his
neighbor" (ibid.; emphasis in original).

[37] *VS* 13.

[38] *VS* 90–94. For a reflection on its value see Joseph Ratzinger, "The
Renewal of Moral Theology: Perspectives of Vatican II and *Veritatis splendor*",
Communio International Catholic Review 32, no. 2 (Summer 2005).

[39] See Paolo Martinelli, *La testimonianza: Verità di Dio e libertà dell'uomo*
(Milan: Paoline, 2002).

beyond any norm, although the norm itself preserves it.[40] Therefore the good of the person is the foundation of the moral law, and not vice versa. This is why someone who thinks that moral problems can be resolved only by changing the norm commits a grave error. This manifests a blatant legalism that claims to measure moral good only by the law. Moreover, experience teaches very clearly that someone who does not respect institutional norms is someone who immediately imposes his own subjective norms.

The gospel of the family has a lot to do with this "creative truth of love", since it shows the enormous capacity of the familial community to respond to difficulties and also to transform them into an occasion for greater union among its members. This can never be dictated by a law, which, however, does not change the fact that there are acts that can never be good. In this sense Kasper is right when he says that "the mere question of what is permitted and what is forbidden doesn't help any further."[41] It is not enough to know what *cannot be done*; it is necessary to blaze trails of positive acts that really help people.

Inasmuch as it has cognitive significance, the virtue of prudence seeks what is best in every action. The beginning of the action does not lie in the formulation of a norm, but rather in the attraction of the concrete goods with their specific value;[42] in this sense prudence is the virtue that avoids legalism of any sort, even the legalism of those who

[40]See Livio Melina, "'Bene della persona' e 'beni per la persona'", *Lateranum* 77 (2011): 89–107.

[41] *Gospel of the Family*, p. 49.

[42]For a magnificent study on prudence, see Livio Melina, *La conoscenza morale: linee di riflessione sul Commento di san Tommaso all'Etica Nicomachea*, 2nd ed. (Milan: EDUCatt, 2005).

continually look for exceptions to norms; as a knowledge of the good, prudence can be closely correlated with charity, which increases its epistemological value.[43]

5.4. The Legalistic View of Seeking Exceptions

It is obvious that marriage has become the center of proposals for pastoral "creativity", due to the cultural opposition that exists and because of the notion that it is very difficult to live out the Gospel ideal of the family in a world that is so far removed from it. We should not be surprised that a whole literature has emerged that continually seeks these exceptions. Pope Benedict XVI brings this aspect to light and reveals its origin:

> Mercy, Equity, the *Oikonomia* so dear to the Oriental Tradition, are some of the concepts invoked in such interpretative operations. It is immediately appropriate to note that this framework does not overcome the Positivism which it denounces, limiting itself to replacing it [Positivism] with another in which interpretive human work rises to the level of protagonist in establishing that which is juridical. It lacks the meaning of an objective law which one is to seek, because it remains at the mercy of considerations which claim to be theological or pastoral, but in the end are exposed to the risk of arbitrariness.[44]

---

[43] See C. A. J. van Ouwerkerk, *Caritas et ratio: Étude sur le double principe de la vie morale chrétienne d'après S. Thomas d'Aquin* (Nijmegen: Drukkerij Gebr. Janssen, 1956).

[44] "Address of His Holiness Benedict XVI for the Inauguration of the Judicial Year of the Tribunal of the Roman Rota", January 21, 2012.

Kasper himself has repeated these warnings,[45] but as usual, once he states a principle to show that he knows it, he seeks other ways out. The only way to understand why, in the address that we are analyzing, there is such an accumulation of references to distinct and very different logics is that they have one aim: to find exceptions to a norm. It is impossible to overlook the enormous ambiguity with which this topic is discussed. The Cardinal mixes the spiritual discernment that he attributes to Saint Alphonsus and Saint Benedict[46] with Saint Thomas' virtue of prudence[47] and with his distinction between theoretical and practical reason, and he goes so far as to speak about the primacy of wisdom[48] and to correlate it with *oikonomia*, mercy, and *epikeia*.[49] This invocation of every sort of virtue is done in a rather eclectic and disorderly fashion but, one must admit, with a key objective: to justify an exception to a law in theological terms, thus tying in with the strategy of doubt that we spoke about in chapter 2.

Obviously, given such a blend of different references, it is impossible to clarify their substance in the least. We already spoke about mercy with respect to truth and justice, and about the value of *oikonomia* as revelation, and, in both cases, we sought to provide a theological explanation that goes far beyond being a mere criterion for applying

[45] Kasper discusses the preceding passage in his *Mercy: The Essence of the Gospel and the Key to Christian Life*, trans. William Madges (New York/Mahwah, N.J.: Paulist Press, 2013), p. 178–79.

[46] See *Gospel of the Family*, pp. 46 and 41, n. 21, respectively.

[47] Cited in *Gospel of the Family*, pp. 33–34; he cited the sources in Saint Thomas' works at notes 21–23, p. 41, with reference to Thomas' distinction between speculative reason and practical reason; another reference is on p. 46.

[48] Ibid., pp. 29, 33.

[49] On *epikeia*, see ibid., pp. 46, 50, again in reference to *oikonomia*.

a law. Something similar happened with prudence and wisdom, as virtues that correspond to an eminent exercise of reason. The literature about these two themes is very extensive, in particular in relation to Saint Thomas.[50] Even a minimal study of these virtues must be based on the acceptance by the Angelic Doctor of the existence of acts that are intrinsically evil because of their object and therefore not allow exceptions.[51]

Nevertheless, the main question is one of the topics taken up by Pope Benedict in his discourse, which the Cardinal, though, does not take into consideration. His insistence on seeking exceptions to a law is a *legalistic* way of considering the law. In this case, the law is considered to be primarily restrictive and is not understood as a guide of human actions. He therefore follows a nominalist vision of the law as essentially coming from an authority (*bonum quia iussum*) and not from the truth about the good of things (*iussum quia bonum*)—so much so that he thinks that a benevolent change on the part of the authorities could resolve the question.[52] Changing the norm would mean making

[50] The following may serve as reference works: Daniel Westberg, *Right Practical Reason: Aristotle, Action and Prudence in Aquinas* (Oxford: Clarendon Press, 1994); and José Noriega, *"Guiados por el Espíritu": El Espíritu Santo y el conocimiento moral en Tomás de Aquino* (Rome: Mursia, 2000).

[51] This approach is common to the Scholastics, who had to explain it in opposition to Aristotle and with reference to the polemic of Abelard; see John Finnis, *Moral Absolutes: Tradition, Revision and Truth* (Washington, D.C.: Catholic University of America Press, 1991). They did so without losing a vision based on love (Keenan's thesis notwithstanding), as demonstrated by Michael Sherwin, *By Knowledge and by Love: Charity and Knowledge in the Moral Theology of St. Thomas Aquinas* (Washington, D.C.: Catholic University of America Press, 2004).

[52] See the profound reflection by Servais Pinckaers, *The Sources of Christian Ethics*, translated from the third edition by Sr. Mary Thomas Noble (Washington, D.C.: Catholic University of America Press, 1995), pp. 14–17.

the problem cease to exist; introducing a certain exception to an overly rigorous law of indissolubility would mean making sure that everything remains in man's hands and would allow us to resolve the question more humanely.

The legalistic view is incapable of starting from the concrete activity of the human person who is moved by a good and not by the law. In contrast, prudence guides the action interiorly through the accomplishment of the excellent good of the action: the good of the person. It is thus opposed to legalism, which starts from the norm as the principle of judgment and conceives of action only as a concrete case of the norm. Therefore, the problem is determining whether the concrete case corresponds to this norm or to another. These are two completely different ways of understanding action: the first starts from the virtue of prudence, the second from the application of a norm. This is therefore a fundamental difference that we can detect between Saint Thomas Aquinas and Saint Alphonsus Liguori with respect to moral knowledge. Therefore, before citing *both* as sources for the same argument, Kasper ought to have clarified how he understands each of them, because it is difficult to think of a greater irenicism in such a delicate moral question.

All this has a specific application in the case of accepting the state of life of divorced-and-remarried couples. For one way of thinking, this would be a question of mere ecclesiastical law, and the power to change it would belong to the Pope.[53] John Paul II categorically rejected this interpretation, maintaining that this is a question that touches

---

[53] This is the case with Basilio Petrà; see his *Divorziati risposati e seconde nozze nella Chiesa*, pp. 191–205.

upon the faith.[54] Once again, as is obvious, we find ourselves facing a *prior* doctrinal question, which cannot be addressed simply by speaking of a more comprehensive administrative regulation.

5.5. A Peculiar Way of Reasoning

In this anxious search for some possible exception, Cardinal Kasper's address manifests a certain inconsistency, in the following words:

> For such particular cases, the Catholic tradition admittedly does not recognize, like the Orthodox churches, the principle of *oikonomia*, but it does know the similar principle of *epikeia*, the distinguishing of spirits, and equiprobabilism (St. Alphonsus Liguori). It recognizes the Thomistic understanding of the foundational cardinal virtue—prudence—which applies a general norm to the concrete situation (which, in Thomas Aquinas's sense, has nothing to do with situation ethics).[55]

This is the prime example of mixing up references that have some bearing on the distance between the general norm and the concrete case. Naturally, the way of posing the question is very different in the various cases and in the authors to whom he refers. In fact, in the way in which he presents prudence in the writings of Saint Thomas as though it were a mere application of norms to

[54]See "Address of the Holy Father John Paul II to the Tribunal of the Roman Rota", January 21, 2000, no. 8: "The non-extension of the Roman Pontiff's power to ratified and consummated sacramental marriages is taught by the Church's Magisterium as a doctrine to be held definitively."

[55] *Gospel of the Family*, p. 46.

concrete cases, the Cardinal commits an error by not taking into account the many studies that have been written
on the subject in the last forty years, many of them in the
German-speaking world.[56] This sows doubt as to whether
his argument is genuinely based on Aquinas, apart from a
certain lip service. Now, though, what interests us is to
point out the internal structure of his presentation, which
appears paradoxical at least.

In the first place, as is evident in the text, Kasper insists
on the singularity of every case, and, in order to do so,
he resorts to personalist language: "Rather, one must take
seriously the uniqueness of every person and every situation and, case by case, carefully distinguish and decide."[57]
Immediately before that, however, he had to make another
pass antithetical to the one just mentioned: in order to
avoid falling into a sort of casuistry that would completely
undermine his presentation, the Cardinal tries to explain
this singularity as a difficulty in describing cases objectively,[58] in other words, as a question connected with the
value of personal subjectivity.

---

[56] Starting with the book by Wolfgang Kluxen, *Philosophische Ethik bei
Thomas von Aquin* (Hamburg: F. Meiner, 1980), followed by Martin Rhonheimer, *Natur als Grundlage der Moral* (Innsbruck-Vienna: Tyrolia-Verlag,
1987); and Eberhard Schockenhoff, *Bonum hominis: Die anthropologischen und
theologischen Grundlagen der Tugendethik des Thomas von Aquin* (Mainz: Matthias-
Grünewald Verlag, 1987).

[57] *Gospel of the Family*, p. 46. Earlier he resorted to a similar formula when
he said, "Behind every individual legal appeal stands not only a case that can
be viewed through the lens of a general rule, but rather a human person, who
is not only a case, but rather a being who possesses unique personal dignity.
That makes necessary a hermeneutic that is *juridical and pastoral* and that applies
a general law with *prudence and wisdom*, according to justice and fairness, to a
concrete, often complex situation" (ibid., p. 29; emphasis added).

[58] See ibid., p. 45: "There also is not *the* objective situation, which poses an
obstacle to admission to communion, but rather many very different objective
situations.... Therefore, one may not proceed from a concept of the objective situation that has been reduced to one single point" (emphasis in original).

It seems that in doing this he tends toward an error that is common to some forms of moral personalism which, guided by the singular value of the human person, do not perceive the necessary objectivity of the good as a mediation so that intersubjective communication can exist. This is an argument already keenly formulated by Maurice Nédoncelle: "But a person who, in one way or another, does not go through the school of objectivity, is intolerable and disgusting."[59] In reality, we need to distrust an inadequate personalism[60] that is unable to recognize the importance of the common nature that allows human beings to communicate with one another and to discover the existence of a common good that springs from the love to which all human beings are called.[61] Despite the Cardinal's earlier discussion of the natural law,[62] oddly enough, here, where it ought to be pertinent, there is not the least mention of it.

Although the author says explicitly that he intends to distance himself from situation ethics, he does not explain

[59] Cf. Maurice Nédoncelle, *Conscience et logos: Horizons et méthodes d'une philosophie personnaliste* (Paris: Éditions de l'Épi, 1961), p. 40: "Mais la personne qui, sous une forme ou sous une autre, ne passe pas par l'école de l'objectivité, est intolérable et écoeurante." For the necessity of an objective mediation in any personal relation, see Juan José Pérez-Soba, *La pregunta por la persona, la respuesta de la interpersonalidad: Estudio de una categoría personalista* (Madrid: Publicaciones de la Facultad de Teologia "San Dámaso", 2004).

[60] See Juan José Pérez-Soba and Pawel Gałuszka, eds., *Persona e natura nell'agire morale: Memoriale di Cracovia—Studi—Contributi* (Siena: Cantagalli, 2013).

[61] According to the argument of Benedict XVI: "To love someone is to desire that person's good and to take effective steps to secure it. Besides the good of the individual, there is a good that is linked to living in society: the common good" (Encyclical Letter *Caritas in veritate*, June 29, 2009, no. 7).

[62] See *Gospel of the Family*, pp. 5–7. According to his argument, it seems that it must be understood in the sense in which it is used in his address: "a binding gestalt of meaning" (ibid., p. 10).

how he intends to proceed. He cannot do so without recognizing the objectivity of justice. The failure to attribute
due importance to objective, legally determinable elements
leaves the argument in the clouds. This would be a way of
denying *epikeia* itself as a possibility for discernment, since
the objectivity in question is the means that allows the
virtue to judge concretely. No criterion is provided by
which to distinguish his proposal from situation ethics, precisely because in this case he does not follow the
source that he cites, that is, Saint Thomas Aquinas. And
this is why the Cardinal, in his address, when he tries to
determine pastoral solutions, cannot help defining them
by resorting to objective elements after all in order to distinguish the various cases to be addressed. In this instance,
however, he speaks to us about "two situations" that are
different, to which distinct criteria must be applied.[63]

Despite these vacillations, which have anti-juridical
overtones, ultimately, what Kasper is trying to do in his
address is to arrive at *a common norm of action* by means of
a pastoral solution: "Binding criteria should exist and be
publicly identified. I have attempted that in my lecture."[64]
This clearly normative project appears to be logical, since
it is consistent with the opinion that he already expressed
as a theologian: "Legal and pastoral rules or guidelines are
required and these must be clear, unambiguous and possible for everyone to understand."[65] Given these presup-
positions, pastoral ministry necessarily is seen as a source

[63] Ibid., pp. 27–28.

[64] Ibid., p. 52. Therefore, it is necessary to assign this normative sense to
the following phrase in his foreword to his booklet: "to arrive at a hopefully
unanimous response" (p. vi).

[65] Walter Kasper, *Theology of Christian Marriage*, trans. David Smith (New
York: Seabury Press, 1980), p. 69.

of other norms, and, ultimately, the author maintains that a change of norm may be the much-hoped for pastoral solution.

5.6. The Primacy of *Epikeia*: Again a Legalistic View

From what has just been said it becomes evident the desire to define the logic of pastoral vision in terms of the concrete application of general norms is a clear example of the lack of precisely such a vision. This is a model that comes from neo-Scholastic casuistry, which ignored the true dynamic of the human act.[66] It is a question of *perspective*: the one adopted here is that of a judge who must limit someone else's action,[67] yet does not take into account the fact that actions spring from a love that they are supposed to express and in which the person is actualized, as is evident in an authentic personalist vision connected with a metaphysics of love.[68]

If not love but rather the norm is the starting point of one's approach to morality, then the moral law is viewed a priori as a limit, and finding exceptions to it is an expression of freedom. From this limited vision sprang the moral

[66] See Aristide Fumagalli, *Azione e tempo: Il dinamismo dell'agire morale* (Assisi: Cittadella Editrice, 2002).

[67] In order to appreciate the difference between this view and the true moral perspective, see Martin Rhonheimer, *The Perspective of Morality: Philosophical Foundations of Thomistic Virtue Ethics*, trans. Gerald Malsbary (Washington, D.C.: Catholic University of America Press, 2011).

[68] Following is one source of this vision: Karol Wojtyła, *The Acting Person*, trans. Andrzej Potocki (Dordrecht and Boston: D. Reidel, 1979). A study of its personalist approach can be found in Aude Suramy, *La voie de l'amour: Une interprétation de* Personne et acte *de Karol Wojtyła, lecteur de Thomas d'Aquin* (Siena: Cantagalli, 2014).

criteria regarding how to apply norms in relation to the conscience and, consequently, the interminable discussions between rigorists and laxists; this is the interpretive framework within which Kasper's address moves. This is the context in which the equiprobabilism of Saint Alphonsus Liguori originated, to which the Cardinal refers.[69] Nevertheless, overcoming this tension is not achieved by "creating" a new, "spiritualized" sensibility, but rather through a deeper understanding of authentic moral conscience, which is something quite different. The Church's true pastoral care, born of the perception of the truth of love, is decidedly foreign to this whole question. We cannot lose sight of this warning, since, in moral circles, we notice a certain resurgence of casuistry, which is always the consequence of legalism.[70]

This is the context in which there was talk about a greater utilization of *epikeia* in pastoral work. We know very well that the purpose of this attempt is to open up the possibility of an exception to a general norm based on the singularity of a concrete case, as Kasper himself presents it: "*epikeia*, justice in individual cases, which is the higher righteousness, according to Thomas Aquinas".[71] In this way, he echoes Aquinas' categorical statement: "Hence *epikeia* is by way of being [*quasi*] a higher rule of human actions."[72] It appears, therefore, as a reality that promises an open, fair way of dealing with the case in question:

---

[69] See *Gospel of the Family*, p. 46.

[70] See James F. Keenan and Thomas A. Shannon, eds., *The Context of Casuistry* (Washington, D.C.: Georgetown University Press, 1995).

[71] *Gospel of the Family*, p. 50.

[72] *ST* II–II, q. 120, a. 2: "Unde epieikeia est quasi superior regula humanorum actuum."

going beyond the formulation of a law. The Angelic Doctor's argument seems to have a lot to do with the way of presenting things in the address under consideration: "It was not possible to lay down rules of law that would apply to every single case. Legislators in framing laws attend to what commonly happens.... In these [unforeseen] and like cases it is bad to follow the law [to the letter]."[73]

This formula seems to promise new ways of resolving difficulties. Nevertheless, in any case, it is surprising that the German theologian turns to this proposal without offering clarifications, since it was one of the points discussed most extensively in the book of commentaries on the letter from the Congregation for the Doctrine of the Faith about Communion for the divorced and remarried.[74] Those pages explained in great detail the error involved in the attempt to uphold the validity of *epikeia* in cases of this sort.

The clarification in question is very simple: *epikeia* is the specific virtue of the *judge* who must judge a concrete case, and not that of the *legislator* who must compose a norm. This is precisely the origin of the well-known formula that says "[this] is passing judgment not on the law, but on some particular contingency";[75] therefore, "when the case is manifest there is need, not of interpretation, but

[73] *ST* II–II, q. 120, a. 1: "Non fuit possibile aliquam regulam legis institui quae in nullo casu deficeret, sed legislatores attendunt ad id quod in pluribus accidit.... similibus casibus malum esset sequi legem positam."

[74] See Ángel Rodríguez Luño, "Can *epikeia* be used in the pastoral care of the divorced and remarried faithful?", in *L'Osservatore Romano*, Weekly Edition in English, February 9, 2000, p. 9; Piero Giorgio Marcuzzi, "Applicazioni di 'aequitas et epicheia' ai contenuti della Lettera della Congregazione per la Dottrina della Fede del 14 settembre 1994", in Congregation for the Doctrine of the Faith, *Sulla pastorale dei divorziati risposati* (Vatican City: Libreria Editrice Vaticana, 1998), pp. 88–98.

[75] *ST* II–II, q. 120, a. 1, ad 2: "non iudicat de lege, sed de aliquo particulari negotio."

of execution."[76] The specific light of *epikeia* is the same as that of justice, not some other light, but it is different from that of *legal* justice, in other words, from the concrete and imperfect formulation of a human legislator. This is why applying *epikeia* to a specific norm of the natural law is such a thorny issue.

It is worth dwelling on this point, since Kasper, with very little rigor, repeats the idea of Thomistic *epikeia*, but then refers also to Saint Alphonsus Liguori with respect to possible exceptions to a norm. This causes perplexity, since these are very different perspectives, and therefore it would be helpful to know what the Cardinal's real position is with regard to such divergent sources. To take from each one the statements that best support one's own proposal, without any further clarifications, is to adopt an improper sort of theological methodology. This is particularly true because of the difference in their concepts of the natural law. It is clear that in Saint Thomas the *virtue of justice* is more than the expression of a legal determination: "*Epikeia* corresponds properly to legal justice."[77] Therefore, in his view, it is not possible to apply it in the area of natural law. On the contrary, Saint Alphonsus, whose view of the natural law is more voluntarist, must also respond to the difficulty of the Jansenist position, which maintained there could be no inculpable ignorance of any norm of the natural law whatsoever.[78] This is why,

---

[76] *ST* II–II, q. 120, a. 1, ad 3: "in manifestis non est opus interpretatione, sed executione."

[77] *ST* II–II, q. 120, a. 2, ad 1: "epieikeia correspondet proprie iustitiae legali."

[78] See Louis Vereecke, *Da Guglielmo d'Ockham a sant'Alfonso de Liguori: Saggi di storia della teologia morale moderna 1300–1787* (Cinisello Balsamo [MI]: Paoline, 1990), p. 748: "The Jansenist movement, under the influence of the Bayanist doctrine, denied the possibility of invincible ignorance in matters of natural law."

for the patron saint of moralists, *epikeia* can be applied in this area as well, although he then explains it as the variation of a moral object in virtue of a change of concrete circumstances.[79]

To insist, as was already done in the case of mercy, on a "higher justice" specific to *epikeia*, is therefore ambiguous, unless one immediately clarifies the profound reason for that supremacy, which is precisely the intentional value of justice, which cannot be reduced to any legal justice. In this sense, equity is "part of justice".[80]

Here, then, is the appropriate framework for the exercise of *epikeia*: not to make of one's own sensibility a norm, but to turn to the mind of the legislator rather than to the letter of the law. The reason for the exception is therefore as follows: "The legislator himself foresees that if there is a difficulty in applying the law, there is no obligation."[81] This, however, cannot be applied to arguments concerning the natural law, which never depend on the application of a norm composed by a legislator.[82]

---

[79] Clarified by Ángel Rodríguez Luño, in "L'epicheia nella cura pastorale dei fedeli", Congregation for the Doctrine of the Faith, *Sulla pastorale dei divorziati risposati* (Vatican City: Libreria Vaticana, 1998), p. 80.

[80] *ST* II–II, q. 120, a. 2, ad 1: "Si vero iustitia legalis dicatur solum quae obtemperat legi secundum verba legis, sic epieikeia non est pars legalis iustitiae, sed est pars iustitiae communiter dictae, contra iustitiam legalem divisa sicut excedens ipsam." (But if legal justice denotes merely that which complies with the law with regard to the letter, then *epikeia* is a part not of legal justice but of justice in its general acceptation, and is condivided with legal justice, as exceeding it.) *ST* II–II, q. 120, a. 2, ad 2: "epieikeia est melior quadam iustitia, scilicet legali quae observat verba legis. Quia tamen et ipsa est iustitia quaedam, non est melior omni iustitia." (*Epikeia* is better than a certain, namely, legal, justice, which observes the letter of the law; yet since it is itself a kind of justice, it is not better than all justice.)

[81] Gianfranco Ghirlanda, *Il diritto nella Chiesa mistero di comunione* (Cinisello Balsamo [MI]: Paoline, 1993), p. 448.

[82] See Marcuzzi, "Applicazioni di 'aequitas et epicheia'", p. 96.

Therefore, the specific reason for *epikeia* has nothing to do with tolerating an injustice, but rather with the greatest of all justice: "The strict sense of *epikeia* must not be understood according to the logic of exceptions, tolerance or dispensation. *Epikeia* is the principle of an excellent choice and does not mean and has never meant that, by way of exception, it is morally possible to allow a bit of injustice."[83]

The way in which *epikeia* should be applied is very simple: it is necessary to keep clearly in mind *the legal good that is at stake*. Without this clarification, the judgment will not be virtuous but obscured. This is precisely the criterion that Benedict XVI alluded to in his address to the Roman Rota, which Kasper, however, does not take into consideration. The criterion emerges quite naturally:

> In such a manner, a legal hermeneutics which may be authentically juridical is rendered possible, in the sense that, by placing itself in syntony [tune] with the very signification of the law, the crucial question can be posed as to what is just in each case. It would be appropriate to observe, in this respect, that in order to grasp the true meaning of the law one must always seize [i.e., look at and comprehend] the very reality that is being disciplined, and that not only when the law is primarily declarative of the Divine Law, but also when it constitutively introduces human rules. These are, in fact, to be interpreted also in the light of the reality being regulated, which always contains a nucleus of the Natural Law and the Divine Positive Law, with which every norm must be in harmony in order to be rational and truly juridical.[84]

---

[83] Rodríguez Luño, "L'epicheia nella cura pastorale dei fedeli", pp. 80–81.
[84] Benedict XVI, "Address to the Roman Rota", January 21, 2012.

The light that this offers to illuminate the case of cohabiting divorced-and-remarried couples is evident. The law
about the permanence of the matrimonial bond and the
injustice of living in opposition to it turns out to be in
this case quite obvious in the truth of its requirement of
justice. In our case, the prior question of justice to be
clarified is whether or not the person is acting against an
existing sacramental bond. This is not something easy to
determine in concrete cases, but this is precisely the kind
of discernment that must be carried out—not the sort
aimed at understanding whether one needs to be merciful (an aspect that is irrelevant at this level). Once again,
we find ourselves concluding that one cannot consider an
exception to this law as though it were a pastoral question
alone, but rather it is necessary to base one's judgment on
the doctrinal knowledge of an act's authentic value. This
is the true and proper sense of the judicious statement by
Pope Francis: "The juridical dimension and the pastoral
dimension of the Church's ministry do not stand in opposition."[85] Their specific content in the case in question
can be expressed in the words of John Paul II: "In the
Church, true justice, enlivened by charity and tempered
by equity, always merits the descriptive adjective pastoral.
There can be no exercise of pastoral charity that does not
take account, first of all, of pastoral justice."[86]

---

[85] "Address of Pope Francis to the Officials of the Tribunal of the Roman
Rota for the Inauguration of the Judicial Year", January 24, 2014. Cited in
paraphrase in *Gospel of the Family*, pp. 28–29.

[86] "Address of John Paul II to the Tribunal of the Roman Rota", January 18,
1990, no. 4. Thus he clears up a "mistaken idea": "Perhaps it is an understandable one, but not thereby less harmful, for unfortunately it often conditions one's view of the pastoral nature of Church law. This distortion lies in
attributing pastoral importance and intent only to those aspects of moderation

5.7. The Pastoral Approach of the Good Samaritan: Healing the Wounds in the Face of Difficulties

Of course, it is not enough to establish the limits of a law in order to respond to the pastoral challenges that have to do with the weaknesses and wounds of specific persons. This is particularly true in talking about the family. We know very well that for those who want to build a family life, there are many difficulties; we could even say that there are *too* many. It would not be an exaggeration to assert that many Christian families are sick and that the Church's task is to heal them. Nevertheless, in order to be able to carry out this task, it is necessary to make a correct diagnosis, especially when we are talking about an epidemic. The physician, therefore, cannot let himself be taken by the immediacy of the wound, nor by what the sick person asks of him, but must find out above all *the origin of the illness*, because only in that way will he be able to heal the patient. If there is a pandemic, either you attack the hotbed of the infection or else any treatment will be useless.

As we showed in the preceding chapter, the moral malady from which these deficiencies arise relative to the task of forming a family is above all the spread of the *utilitarian, emotivist self*, which, being internally fragmented, is particularly weak at the moment when it tries to build a complete life. We cannot avoid recalling the definition of this kind of personality in order to shed light on our reflections: "Such a human being, while emotional in his

---

and humanness in the law which are linked immediately with canonical equity (*aequitas canonica*)—that is, holding that only the exceptions to the law, the potential non-recourse to canonical procedures and sanctions, and the stream-lining of judicial formalities have any real pastoral relevance" (ibid., no. 3).

interior life, is *utilitarian* with regard to the effective result of his actions, since he is constrained to having this attitude inasmuch as he lives in a technological, competitive world. It is easy to understand, therefore, how complicated it can be for him to perceive adequately the morality of interpersonal relationships, since he interprets them exclusively in a sentimental or utilitarian way."[87]

The great pastoral deficiency, therefore, is to lack an understanding of authentically Christian love, in other words, of love that can structure a *Christian subject* by means of grace. This is certainly due to the Christian family's need to address the educational process of its own children, in which it does not receive enough help to be able to overcome the surrounding contagion of emotivism. Without any real presence of the Christian community, it will be impossible to succeed. It is easy to see the enormous pastoral validity of this principle, for society as well: "The communion of life and love which is marriage thus emerges as an authentic good for society. Today, the need to avoid confusing marriage with other types of unions based on weak love is especially urgent. It is only the rock of total, irrevocable love between a man and a woman that can serve as the foundation on which to build a society that will become a home for all mankind."[88]

This discovery allows us to adopt the right pastoral perspective for considering the various difficult situations

[87] Spanish Episcopal Conference, *Directorio de la pastoral familiar de la Iglesia en España* (Alicante: Ediciones Palabra, 2004), no. 19.

[88] "Address of His Holiness Benedict XVI to Members of the Pontifical John Paul II Institute for Studies on Marriage and Family on the 25th Anniversary of Its Foundation", May 11, 2006. Cf. Livio Melina, *La roccia e la casa: Famiglia, società e bene comune* (Cinisello Balsamo: San Paolo, 2013).

in marriage that, obviously, do not have to do with the divorced and remarried alone. In the first place, we see the originality of the authentically pastoral perspective in contrast with what we have seen until now. This is why we describe such situations as "difficult":

> The pastoral view, however, must be broader, since it cannot be reduced to such a judgment. Starting from what is irregular means ignoring the origin of pastoral activity, in other words, the call heard by the specific person that tends to make him find his own path and not just to adapt to the law. The originality of practical reason, informed by *agape* [*la razionalità pratica e agapica*], enables us not to fall into the temptation to judge cases as though they were merely occasions for applying a norm. That would be tantamount to legalism, which consists in being content to apply the law, without seeking the fullness of the persons' lives. Truth is then understood as a limit that encloses the human being, depriving him of freedom. In this sense, trying to replace a "harsh law" with an "understanding law" adapted to the subject is a grave error. That would simply be exchanging one form of legalism for another, without realizing the fact that this fullness of vocation cannot be expressed by means of a law, but rather precedes it through a call that is inherent in the person's response. Therefore, the truth of love, which includes the encounter with the other, is not a limit of freedom, but rather a privileged occasion for expressing it.[89]

The first consequence of this approach, therefore, is the impossibility of a "gradualness of the law", as Cardinal Kasper himself acknowledges. "This law of gradualness

[89] Pérez-Soba, *La pastorale familare*, p. 155.

seems to me extremely important for marital and familial life and pastoral care. It does not mean gradualness of the law, but rather gradual growth in understanding and carrying out the Gospel law, which is a law of liberty (Jas 1:25; 2:12), which today has often become so difficult for many of the faithful."[90] It is absolutely impossible to make a law for every case; rather, it is necessary to make persons grow so that they may be true Christian subjects. In the case of serious deficiencies, the gradual pastoral approach must be aimed at healing the wounds; therefore it is necessary to diagnose them correctly. It does no good to judge situations, if afterward no type of curative approach is put into practice. Obviously, though, it is even more dangerous to deny the disease and to think that, with a change of norm, the infidelity can cease to exist. In fact, we must keep clearly in mind a pastoral judgment based on well-established experience: the search for "little exceptions" (which presumably are to be controlled) to socially relevant moral laws for the purpose of avoiding extreme situations has *always* had unbridled liberalism as its consequence. The praxis of the Protestant denominations and also of the Orthodox churches confirms this. Therefore the following judgment expressed by the Cardinal appears unrealistic: "The path in question would not be a general

[90]Walter Kasper, *Il vangelo della famiglia* (Brescia: Queriniana, 2014), p. 31. This paragraph is present in the Italian version of Cardinal Kasper's booklet, from which it has been translated here. It is, however, absent in the German edition, on which the English text seems to be based. Cf. *Gospel of the Family*, p. 18: "Marriage and the family, on the path of cross and resurrection (FC 12 f.), stand under the law of gradual development—of growing into the mystery of Christ in a repeatedly new and deeper way (FC 9, 34)." To understand this distinction, see Livio Melina, "Pedagogía moral cristiana: conversión y 'ley de la gradualidad'", in *Moral: entre la crisis y la renovación*, 2nd ed. (Madrid: EIUNSA, 1998), pp. 105–36.

solution. It is not a broad path for the great masses, but a narrow path for the indeed smaller segment of divorced and remarried individuals who are honestly interested in the sacraments."[91]

In the true recovery of persons, in contrast, the real issue at stake is the authentic pastoral approach of charity. Here is a description of the fully merciful logic of the Good Shepherd: "The Church's first duty is to approach these people with love and consideration, with caring and motherly attention, to proclaim the merciful closeness of God in Jesus Christ ... which is addressed to the actual person and sinner that we are, to help us up after any fall and to recover from any injury."[92] The wound after divorce is a serious one, and someone who simply enters a new marriage aggravates it, but access to Holy Communion is not the medicine. Instead it is necessary to devote much attention to the whole family, starting with the most innocent victims, the children.[93] The moral illness that appears in these trials is connected with other serious pastoral issues that must be addressed also.

In this context reference is made to the penitential nature of Christian life.[94] All who do pastoral work in this field agree in recognizing the necessity of a penitential path to accompany the situation of the divorced and remarried—something which in fact is being done in many places, at

[91] *Gospel of the Family*, pp. 32–33.

[92] "Address of His Holiness Benedict XVI to Participants in an International Congress Organized by the John Paul II Institute for Studies on Marriage and Family", April 5, 2008.

[93] See Livio Melina and C. A. Anderson, eds., *L'olio sulle ferite: Una risposta alle piaghe dell'aborto e del divorzio* (Siena: Cantagalli, 2009).

[94] The foundations are laid and a penitential path is described in *Gospel of the Family*, pp. 30–32.

least in Italy.[95] This kind of practice is useful so that no one feels left alone but rather is accompanied by the ecclesial community. The goal, however, should be to lead to an acknowledgment of the truth of one's own situation so that some response can be made to the requirements of the indissoluble conjugal covenant. Listing these steps with precision and creating programs of this sort is no doubt highly advantageous.[96] In doing so, there is no pretense of "inventing" an exception to the requirement of the indissolubility of valid, ratified, and consummated marriages; the intention, rather, is to provide an appropriate response to "what God has joined". Along these lines, it is much more urgent to consider the change involved in a pastoral approach of accompaniment which has scarcely taken its first steps.

Hence we see the necessity for an approach that looks to the *future* and bears upon an *integral marriage preparation* without forgetting the merciful vision born of charity

[95] See the well-grounded essays collected in Paolo Gentili, Tommaso Cioncolini, and Giulia Cioncolini, eds., National Office of the Italian Episcopal Conference for Pastoral Care to the Family, *Luci di speranza per la famiglia ferita: Persone separate e divorziati risposati nella comunità cristiana* (Siena: Cantagalli, 2012).

[96] Interesting steps are proposed by Xavier Lacroix, ed., in "Face au divorce", *Oser dire le mariage indissolubile* (Paris: Cerf, 2001), pp. 229–30:

The principal moments could be the following:

   – acknowledgment of having transgressed an important commandment of the Lord;
   – acknowledgment of a lack of fidelity to the oneness implied in the sacrament of matrimony;
   – acknowledgment of the wrongs done and the sins committed, especially against the spouse and the children of the first union, with reparation when possible;
   – words of reconciliation and forgiveness offered to the first spouse;
   – acknowledgment of the mysterious permanence of the first bond;
   – the firm resolution to live out the present bond while heeding the Gospel.

which can see in shortcomings an opportunity to manifest the presence of grace.

5.8. The Lack of Preparation

When one adopts the merciful view that sees the short-comings of the human heart, the first thing that appears is the current lack of adequate preparation for marriage in many places. Anyone who comes into contact with marriage-related pastoral care complains about it. Although it is valuable to organize and conduct premarital courses, their inadequacy is clearly understood in comparison with any other catechumenal process. One commonly hears it said that if at least seven years of preparation are required in order to enter the priesthood, then reducing the preparation for marriage to a few days is too drastic.

That is one way of calling attention to an inadequate model, yet it is not an appropriate response, since it is based on the incorrect application of a merely sacramental model that does not notice the originality of the sacrament of matrimony inasmuch as it is anchored in the reality of creation. A person prepares for marriage *from birth*, because he learns in his own family what a father is and what a mother is, the nature of their union and the richness of the vocation to marriage. The internal weakness of families in transmitting the faith—in other words, the great difficulty that they have in their mission of education—is the main factor in the personal deficiencies encountered at the moment when the sacrament of matrimony is contracted.[97]

[97] A point highlighted by Giuseppe Angelini, in *Educare si deve ma si può?* (Milan: Vita e Pensiero, 2002).

The Church, in her evangelization, must take seriously the unique mission that is hers: *to teach every person to love.* This pastor's insight illumined the whole life of John Paul II and led him to declare: "It is necessary to prepare young people for marriage, it is necessary *to teach them love.* Love is not something that is learned, and yet there is nothing else as important to learn! *As a young priest I learned to love human love.*"[98]

This preparation requires knowing how to accompany a vocation to love. Certainly, this vision was one of the major contributions of *Familiaris consortio*, but it must also be considered as one of the greatest shortcomings of pastoral care to families in our time. The three stages proposed by the Apostolic Exhortation—remote, proximate, and immediate[99]—must truly be implemented throughout the Church. It is not possible to accomplish all this without a profound change of structures, especially with regard to the catechesis of children, pastoral care in schools, and youth ministry. An authentically pastoral perspective identifies this as a profound path for ecclesial renewal, with many implications that must be put into practice.[100]

One essential aspect of this perspective is *faith with respect to marriage,* since the imposing secularizing force of our present-day culture acts in such a manner as to deny on many occasions that there is any *natural* dimension of

[98] John Paul II, *Crossing the Threshold of Hope* (New York: Alfred A. Knopf, 1994), pp. 122–23. See also Livio Melina and Stanislaw Grygiel, eds., *Amare l'amore umano: L'eredità di Giovanni Paolo II sul Matrimonio e la Famiglia* (Siena: Cantagalli, 2007).

[99] See *FC* 66.

[100] See Ramón Acosta Peso, *La luz que guía toda la vida: La vocación al amor, hilo conductor de la pastoral familiar* (Madrid: Edice, 2007).

marriage, such as its sacred character. Kasper refers to this issue as the first of the situations to be taken into consideration,[101] and it had previously been emphasized by Benedict XVI.[102]

In particular, the pastorally most relevant aspect at this time is renewed attention to couples during their first years of marriage. Indeed, the overwhelming majority of separations occur in this first phase. Couples, however, do not perceive the Church as a help in these initial difficulties. While anybody who has serious economic needs knows that he can always turn to the Church, a couple that is having problems does not see the ecclesial community as a place of effective support. This is probably *the* greatest pastoral challenge for the Church in relation to the gospel of the family—a vast field that the Synod must address.[103] It would be pharisaical to say that we are paying a lot of attention to the divorced, when instead we did not support them during the process of separation.

5.9. By Way of a Conclusion: Hope in a Charity That Does Not Disappoint

We see, therefore, that the difficult situations are symptoms of serious shortcomings in our way of understanding and living out Christian love. Overcoming these weaknesses must therefore be the first criterion for a comprehensive

[101] See *Gospel of the Family*, pp. 27–28.

[102] See "Address of His Holiness Benedict XVI for the Inauguration of the Judicial Year of the Tribunal of the Roman Rota", January 26, 2013.

[103] The following is highly recommended as a comprehensive reflection on the topic: Livio Melina, ed., *I primi anni di matrimonio: La sfida pastorale di un periodo bello e difficile* (Siena: Cantagalli, 2014).

pastoral action. Naturally, treating these wounds is possible only if there is adequate *overall* pastoral care that cannot focus solely on one of the problems.

The perspective that we should adopt—in other words, the truer pastoral view—is, ultimately, similar to the one Cardinal Kasper suggests, although he does not examine it in sufficient depth: the perspective that he defines as doing "the truth in love" (Eph 4:15). Its importance consists in the fact that it involves the epistemology of love outlined in the Encyclical *Lumen fidei* by Pope Francis.[104] The characteristics of the pastoral care of the family follow, therefore, from this logic and exist only insofar as they correspond to it. Their value as witness will be sufficiently eloquent for the Church and for the whole world, always with reference to the decisive importance of the vocation to love, as the Pope declares:

> Encountering Christ, letting themselves be caught up in and guided by his love, enlarges the horizons of existence, gives it a firm hope which will not disappoint. Faith is no refuge for the fainthearted, but something which enhances our lives. It makes us aware of a magnificent calling, the vocation of love. It assures us that this love is trustworthy and worth embracing, for it is based on God's faithfulness which is stronger than our every weakness.[105]

At this point we cannot refrain from giving an initial indication of what this perspective implies with regard to the principal difficulties in marriage:

[104] There is a study on this topic in Juan José Pérez-Soba, *Creer en el amor: Un modo de conocimiento teológico* (Madrid: BAC, 2014).

[105] *LF* 53. This is the conclusion of the reflection on the value of the common good of faith, precisely the part in which there is reference to the family.

The look of mercy, therefore, makes us see the difficult situations not as problems to be resolved technically, but rather invites us to discover in them the serious shortcomings of human love that need to be healed. The homosexual question is, in the first place, a difficulty in assuming one's sexual identity; cohabiting couples—a lack of hope with respect to the promise of the "forever" which transforms love into a covenant; separations—a weakness in the everyday reality of conjugal charity as a light by which to build a life together; and the question of divorce—the inability to see indissolubility as a grace and not as an imposition.[106]

This brings into focus the most serious challenges for the family today, but from a perspective that looks at the roots of the illness that is to be healed, a perspective that is concerned with the formation of the moral subject and is not limited to finding a normative solution. We see how it is correlated first and foremost with the "abundant life" proclaimed by the Good Shepherd. We can say that in some places this perspective is being implemented, and the results are truly positive.

Certainly, this is a profound change in our way of thinking about pastoral care: one fundamental aspect of the pastoral care of the family is precisely recognizing that where humanly speaking only a shortcoming is visible, this becomes the occasion for a marvelous manifestation of God's grace.[107] One of the clearest manifestations of

[106] See Juan José Pérez-Soba, "La pastoral familiar, una llamada a toda la Iglesia", *Familia et vita* 19, no. 1 (2014). A fuller development of the topic can be found in *Pastorale familiare*, pp. 151–91.

[107] See Juan José Pérez-Soba, ed., *"Saper portare il vino migliore": Strade di pastorale familiare* (Siena: Cantagalli, 2014).

the mercy of the heart of Christ is the sign of the *wedding feast of Cana*. Marriage appears therefore as a special place of mercy because of its vulnerability, since it runs the risk of losing the wine of joy. This is where Jesus Christ acts to reveal his status as the Bridegroom and thus gives the Church the ability to transform into wine what was merely the water of disenchantment. This is the very first sign of his messianic mission, from which the disciples' faith was born (see Jn 2:11). It is therefore a fundamental paradigm for the pastoral perspective that we are concerned with. Saint Thomas Aquinas takes this Gospel passage as an example of mercy, and in it he of course highlights Mary's intervention: "Now, since the Blessed Virgin was full of mercy, she wanted to alleviate the distress of others."[108] This is the font of grace from which we should draw.

---

[108] Saint Thomas Aquinas, *In Ioannem*, c. 2, lect. 1, no. 345: "Quia ergo virgo beata misericordia plena erat, defectus aliorum sublevare volebat." Kasper refers to this passage in *Mercy*, p. 23.

CONCLUSION

A Gospel, Rather Than a Problem

We have made a brief survey of the theme for the Synod, following the thread of the questions raised by Cardinal Kasper's address. We have tried to discuss the sensitive points with sufficient seriousness, albeit briefly, so as to reveal the complexity that they involve and to avoid any simplification that does not help to realize the situations that exist. This is the service that we thought that we should offer with a view to the Synod of Bishops within the context of a public debate that can be greatly enriching.

The unifying theme that we have sought to follow is to see the centrality of the family as good news in the Church's pastoral care. We must admit that this is surely a desire rather than a reality, since our pastoral structures are very far from responding to the elementary requirements of the cultural challenge that the Church must meet. This is the first of our conclusions: it is necessary to grasp the cultural key if one is really to understand the Church's situation with regard to the gospel of the family. Only in this way will it be possible to understand adequately the reality of persons, above and beyond the sociological data.

This is why the gospel of the family must be understood as the principal point of reference for all pastoral care. Therefore we must avoid the temptation to focus the Synod artificially on one question and make it the key point without which this assembly would not make sense. This is not a mere stratagem, but it corresponds to the specific reason for the existence of the family, which has to do with the *mystery of human identity* and cannot be reduced to a problem.[1] Thus we discover the central role of the family at the heart of God's plan as a reality included in the kerygma, and precisely for this reason it must be present in any evangelization, so as to influence the way in which its characteristics are set forth, as the Gospel teaches us. This is due to the fact that the family contains a fundamental *truth* about man, which can never be forgotten and which is endangered nowadays. Indeed, as John Paul II himself, the "pope of the family",[2] taught us in his catecheses on the theology of the body,[3] this plan of God for the family reveals to human beings their vocation to love, which they discover in Christ; in this vocation they recognize themselves as created through love, redeemed through love, and called to love.

Already in the early Church this was one of the things that distinguished Christians from the pagan world that surrounded them, which was characterized by an aggressively sexualized culture that was prone to divorce, whereas the faithful understood very clearly what was required of

---

[1] As pointed out by Gabriel Marcel in his *Being and Having*, trans. Katharine Farrer (Westminster: Dacre Press, 1949), p. 100: "It is a proper character of problems, moreover, to be reduced to detail. Mystery, on the other hand, is something which cannot be reduced to detail." For a study, see F. Blázquez Carmona, *La filosofía de Gabriel Marcel: De la dialéctica a la invocación* (Madrid: Encuentro, 1988), 157–84.

[2] "Holy Mass and Rite of Canonization of Blesseds John XXIII and John Paul II: Homily of Pope Francis", April 27, 2014.

[3] See John Paul II, *Man and Woman He Created Them: A Theology of the Body*, trans. Michael Waldstein (Boston: Pauline Books and Media, 2006).

them—even though it was contrary to the customs of their age—and devoted due attention to the concrete cases to which they assigned importance and legal relevance.

Consequently, proclaiming and living out the gospel of the family is a fundamental path to follow for the New Evangelization, since on this path one discovers and witnesses to the strength of the Christian family as a subject that conveys the Gospel. The family has experienced an enormous capacity to generate culture—a culture that permeates the life of persons. By means of education, the family is in a position to structure the Christian subject who is able to live out in its fullness the vocation to which God is calling him.

In this good news, mercy is an essential dimension, both for understanding it and for the pastoral activity on the part of the Church. The very revelation of God's design for marriage and the family is closely connected with the manifestation of God as merciful, which is directly related to the fulfillment of his covenant. The gift of divine mercy is fully realized with the forgiveness accomplished in Christ, in his Incarnation and redemption, full of grace and truth (see Jn 1:14). It follows that the real meaning of divine mercy cannot be defined as compassion or tolerance but goes much further. God's grace makes us capable of fidelity and forgiveness. Just as baptism is the expression of a definitive covenant in Christ, so too the indissolubility of marriage, which is a reality of the order of creation, acquires its own definitive value as a sacrament of the New Covenant.

Thus, we have tried to show the error involved in the attempts to relativize indissolubility or to look for exceptions to it, whether these attempts are based on a false view of mercy, on a so-called *oikonomia*, on the virtue of *epikeia*, on prudence, wisdom, or spiritual discernment. The patristic foundation for a praxis of tolerance with regard to the reception of Holy Communion for the divorced and remarried is far from clear, and it is not sufficient grounds for a change of the discipline of the Catholic Church in this matter, which is based on solid doctrinal reasons and not on a rigorist choice of the Latin Church. Any variation of this discipline, therefore, will have to explain, doctrinally, its understanding of the matrimonial bond, which is the foundation of love and justice for any pastoral care of the family.

Going beyond Kasper means precisely to invite Catholics to take the step that he did not take, in other words, to move from a description of the beauty of the gospel of the family to its ability to transform the Church's pastoral ministry, the moral subject, and the surrounding culture. This is certainly a vision of a New Evangelization. If we want the Synods really to confront the challenges that contemporary culture poses for the family, we need to adopt a broader and more pastoral perspective than the one that the Cardinal presented in his address. We explained that trying to resolve a pastoral problem solely through the change of a norm is an error and a masked legalism. With such a practice, the law is eventually left up to subjective caprice, and experience teaches that any presumed control over its application cedes to the effective absence of any limits whatsoever. Protestant and Orthodox practice proves this very clearly, and from these examples we should learn the appropriate lessons.

Family, become what you are, is the call to identity expressed by John Paul II during the preceding Synod on the family.[4] It is an appeal to the future and to a trust in God's mercy, in which we must believe. The entire evangelization of the Church consists in "believing in Jesus Christ, come in the flesh", and the indissoluble union of spouses in "one flesh" is an exalted expression thereof; this is where we discover the vocation to love that springs from the love of a Father and is generated and increased by the gift of the Spirit, who pours out charity into our hearts (cf. Rom 5:5) as a "[l]ove [that] never ends" (1 Cor 13:8). This is the grace received, which is capable of redeeming man and making him capable of the indissoluble covenant with God. In the "flesh" of Christ in which spouses are united, they find, thanks to the Father's mercy, the foundation for their faithfulness. This is the faith that illumines the gospel of the family and that should inspire the upcoming Synods.

[4]See *FC* 17.

APPENDIX

Thirty Key Questions for the
Synods on the Family

I. The Challenge of the Pansexualist Culture

1. What is currently the real challenge for the Christian family?

At this moment the most important challenge for the family is a **cultural** one. As a result of the sexual revolution in the 1960s, there was a change in the way of thinking about sexuality. An ideology became widespread that weakens the understanding of the family, because it compares it to what are supposedly other familial models and makes it difficult for persons to experience what their heart truly desires: a real family.

The results of sociological studies show us in fact that the family, as understood by the Church, is by far the institution most highly appreciated by the people in many countries, although it is culturally opposed. Clearly, this is the most important point about which the Church will have to speak out in her work of evangelization; otherwise she runs the risk of causing a short circuit between what she says and what people understand and live. Observers have emphasized a connection between the crisis of the family and the weakening of the faith.

2. *What is a "sexual revolution"? How many have there been over the course of history?*

A **sexual revolution** is a radical cultural change in the way of understanding the relations between a man and a woman, and in the fundamental meanings of the difference between the sexes in all that pertains to their union of love and to procreation.

If we consider those that occurred during the Christian era, we find in the first place the moral and sexual revolution of Hellenism that was confronted by the primitive Church. Next we must mention the one in the twelfth century, at the time of the transition between the Low and the High Middle Ages and the Gnostic influence of the Cathari and the Albigensians, which gave rise to courtly love that was always adulterous. At the beginning of the Renaissance there was an exaltation of some pagan behaviors connected with a form of sensuality without transcendence. The Enlightenment produced a cynical sort of libertinism; its influence extended to the Romantic movement, which very strongly criticized marriage, describing it as a "prison of love". In the twentieth century, in parallel with the Communist revolution in the Soviet Union, which considered the family to be a bourgeois invention, there was the sexual revolution in the twenties in Western countries that championed an ideological separation between the body, considered to be a biological component without any other significance, and the personal sphere, which can impose any kind of meaning on the body.

The sexual revolution of the sixties in the twentieth century gave rise to the current pansexual culture.

3. *What is pansexualism? How can the Church respond to it?*

Pansexualism is an ideological conception of sexuality that is becoming increasingly widespread and permeating our whole society. What it proposes is simple: (1) reduce sexuality to sex, in other words, to sexual excitation, without any other meanings; (2) introduce sexuality into the consumer society, so that it becomes an object of exchange at all levels; and (3) consider this reality as a positive achievement, as social progress that is capable of liberating persons.

Everything changes when we consider sexuality as a personal dimension through which persons communicate and establish steady relationships. One cannot conduct commerce with persons, nor with emotions. The Church must know how to offer the gospel of marriage and of the family as a profound truth about the human person, an "adequate anthropology", as Saint John Paul II, the "pope of the family", called it in his *Theology of the Body*. In it we find a clear language and a way of overcoming pansexualism.

4. *What does it mean to be an emotivist subject? Why does an emotivist subject meet with so many difficulties in his marriage?*

Emotivism is an inadequate way of thinking about the identity of the personal subject. The emotivist person identifies with his emotions to the point of evaluating the morality of his actions according to the emotions that they arouse in him. An action is good if it "feels good", and it is bad if it "feels bad". This is a sort of moral relativism that has permeated the conscience, as John Henry Cardinal Newman had prophetically foreseen. Emotivism denies any sort of objective reason that could guide the person in his moral judgments, but above all, it confines a human being to the brief duration of his changing emotions, which collide with and contradict one another.

The emotivism of our era is transmitted by the educational system, which fails to educate the affections, and by the prevalence of a false idea of autonomy, which leaves a person the prisoner of his emotions as the sole criterion in life.

An emotivist person has great difficulty understanding life as a whole, because emotion falsifies time, which is always viewed as an enemy; it disrupts space as well, given that it fragments the person into distinct areas of life. An emotivist subject is different during his free time, with his friends, when he is at home and at work, etc. Furthermore, emotivism prevents the person from learning lessons from his experiences, which are always simply judged to be positive or negative, without any grasp of their meaning. Emotivism therefore produces what is described as "affective illiteracy", which prevents us from understanding what the affections have to tell us when it comes to building our life and its story.

This is a true disorder of the personality, an illness in the proper sense, which must be healed in order for someone to be adequately equipped to embark on marriage. Therefore it becomes clear that a true **affective education** is needed, which permits persons to integrate their emotions and feelings, with all the positive things that they convey, into a path of love gradually, as they find their way through the personal ties that result from them. In the Church's tradition there are authors who have appraised the affections in a very positive way, considering them as a language of God, and for this reason the Church has a great wealth of human and divine wisdom to offer in this area.

5. *To what extent does the fact that couples marry with adolescent personalities and with a romantic idea of love become a pastoral problem?*

The reality of the emotivist subject is the reason for the excessive duration of adolescence in our Western society. It follows that persons come to the point of marriage with an **adolescent mentality** that is incapable of taking responsibility for the real difficulties of living together.

This fragility is aggravated by the romantic interpretation of the love between a man and a woman, which prevents them from seeing the true source of spousal love.

The combination of these two realities greatly weakens couples in their efforts to start a life together according to God's plan, because they are building their life on sand and are still exposed to external circumstances which, on many occasions, are hostile to them.

In order to overcome these deficiencies, pastoral accompaniment is necessary; a simple course of marriage preparation is not enough. The Church must offer follow-up care in order to resolve problems, knowing that for modern couples it is very difficult to ask for help. We must reflect on why so many couples have the impression that the Church is distant from their real problems, precisely at the moment in which it would be most urgent to address them pastorally.

6. *Why is romantic love incompatible with marriage?*

Romantic love originated as a cultural response to a type of rationalism that ignored the affections, and it is no accident that it appears to be an irrational emotional explosion. According to the romantic understanding, love is something purely *spontaneous*, detached from any obligation, and its authenticity is measured solely by the standard of its *intensity*. When these conditions are present, time becomes the enemy of love, because it consumes it from within and pursues it until it puts an end to it. Finally, romantic love overvalues *intimacy*, and it is limited to the perimeter that surrounds the couple and stubbornly resists any outside help.

Marriage as an institution and a social reality therefore becomes the enemy of love because it locks it into obligations formulated in positive legal norms.

Christianity, in contrast, believes that love is an act of freedom that concerns the whole person, and that the truth thereof resides in the good that *it promises*, and not in the intensity with which it is felt. This is why the formula of consent to marry is a promise. The matrimonial bond, consequently, arises from the exchange of promises pronounced in the presence of a higher authority, before God himself. For this reason, time helps couples to understand that the source of the love of husband and wife is found in a greater Love that surpasses them, and this Love is what gives them the solid rock on which to build a steady relationship supported by the divine gift.

II. Mercy and the Church's Pastoral Care

7. *What is the difference between mercy and compassion?*

Mercy is the greatest of the divine attributes because it tells us about the interior life of God. We can have access to its most authentic meaning only through the revelation that God has given to mankind in history.

In it, the attribute of mercy appears as *faithfulness to the covenant*, despite man's unfaithfulness. In this revelation, man's greatest misfortune is to live apart from the covenant. Returning to the covenant is the real content of the salvation that God promises to the believer.

Compassion, in contrast, denotes the affective reaction that enables us to go beyond our own feelings so as to take on those of another person. This is especially important with regard to suffering, from within a human perspective. Mercy far surpasses mere compassion because it shows us, out of the immense depths of the divine omnipotence, that God is able to overcome all human miseries, especially those associated with sin and death.

8. *Why should we distinguish mercy from tolerance?*

Tolerance results from the difficulty of coexisting with evil. We must tolerate some evils so as to be able to persevere in our search for the good, because experience teaches us that otherwise we run into greater evils. **Mercy**, on the other hand, does not speak about tolerance of evil but about victory over it.

It is true that love for a person makes us tolerate his defects, but always with the desire that he might succeed in overcoming them, inasmuch as we want the greatest good for that person. Mercy, unlike mere tolerance, *forgives the evil*, freely giving a love that surpasses the offense and makes reconciliation possible.

We see therefore the fundamental difference: a merely tolerant God would not be affected by our offenses; his distance from our little world would make him indifferent to them. A merciful God, in contrast, is one who is offended by our acts and wants to heal us of the evil that results from being separated from our covenant with him. He is a surprisingly close God who overcomes any and all compromises with evil.

In a radically individualistic world like ours, in which respect alone is proposed as the highest norm for human relations, we are easily tempted to confuse mercy and tolerance, although that is actually a falsification of mercy.

9. *What does Saint Thomas Aquinas mean when he says that mercy is the "highest justice"?*

What Saint Thomas Aquinas means when he says that mercy is the "highest justice" is that God never forgets **justice** and that he, the Almighty, guarantees justice among human persons. Therefore there is no such thing as unjust mercy that violates justice, because that would harm personal dignity.

Justice is so important that in the Bible it takes on a transcendent value; indeed, it means to live according to the will of God, to "conform" to his will. This opens up for us a broader perspective than human justice—the mercy that springs from the depths of God's love—and it can accomplish what justice alone is incapable of doing. In other words, it can completely repair the offense committed and reconcile the sinner.

This is why, whereas the blood of Abel cries out for justice, Christ's blood grants mercy and fulfills Abel's request in an excellent way (cf. Heb 12:24).

There is no greater falsification of mercy than the one that claims a nonexistent right to act against justice, even if moved by compassion.

10. *Is looking for exceptions to a moral law consistent with an adequate pastoral approach of mercy?*

Looking for exceptions to a moral law is a distortion of mercy and shows a lack of understanding for the moral significance of the law, inasmuch as it is confused with a positive human law. The reason for this is a sort of **legalism** that sees the law merely as the imposition of the legislator's will, something that by nature is subject to different interpretations and therefore open to occasional **exceptions**. This is Ockham's position: "An act is good because it is commanded; it is bad because it is forbidden" (*bonum quia iussum, malum quia prohibitum*). In reality, the law is the expression of a truth about the good that guides our actions toward union with God. As Saint Thomas declared: "An act is commanded because it is good; it is forbidden because it is bad" (*iussum quia bonum, prohibitum quia malum*). This is why there can be no exceptions to this truth but merely clarifications of its content.

Mercy, as such, is "higher" than any law, because there is always the possibility of a greater good that can never be subordinated to the commandment. But mercy cannot be considered as a means for going against the law, that is, for excusing an evil. This is why the logic of mercy always requires it to overcome evil and not to conceal it or to minimize its importance.

The human authority that imposes laws reserves for itself the option of limiting the extent of its command in order to show its benevolence; in doing this it shows its imperfection, because it cannot claim to take every particular case into consideration. The divine authority, in contrast, employs mercy to make a human person capable of the good contained in its commands. In many cases, in going beyond its role of service, the compassion of a human authority tends to exalt itself; God, however, lifts up the lowly, by making the sinner just.

11. *Are there cases in which it is possible to deny someone forgiveness or mercy?*

According to the teaching of Jesus, as we see in particular in the parable of the good Samaritan, mercy is universal and active, inasmuch as it contains the imperative "Go and do likewise." No one is excluded from the gift of mercy, inasmuch as "the earth is full" of it (Ps 33:5), nor from the resulting offer of forgiveness. We are talking about a divine gift that must always be offered (Mt 18:22), even to enemies (Mt 5:44). It is a gift to which we can never apply a human limit.

Inasmuch as they are divine gifts, mercy and forgiveness need to be accepted by all human persons. It is here that they can come up against human refusal that for some reason makes them impossible. Someone who has not truly repented in his heart and who does not sincerely reject his sin cannot receive forgiveness. In the same way, mercy cannot really be received when the evil is not overcome, when there is no conversion of the one to whom it is offered.

In these cases, it may appear as if forgiveness or mercy were denied to a person, but in reality it is the person himself who renders himself incapable of receiving it.

III. The Divorced and "Civilly Re-Married" or Those Who Live in a New Union

12. *Why is it not possible to give absolution to someone who is divorced and remarried, whereas it is possible to give it to other sinners? Is this not a form of discrimination?*

The impossibility of giving absolution to the divorced and remarried is precisely an example of what we explained before: a priest can never give **absolution to a sinner** who has not really repented. True repentance is not mere displeasure about what has happened and about the consequences; it is a rejection of the sinful action and the necessary detachment from it. The sacrament of penance always requires a true conversion: turning away from sin and uniting with God.

The sin committed by a divorced person when he has sexual relations with another person who is not his spouse is the sin of adultery, according to the definition thereof that Jesus gives in the Gospel (see Mt 19:9) and the testimony of Saint Paul to the disciples (cf. Rom 7:3). Repenting of this sin means not just being sorry about the separation, which in some cases may be irreversible, but truly rejecting a sinful sexual union in the present situation, regardless of whether or not the person was to blame for the breakup of the first relationship. If this does not happen, there is no leeway for receiving absolution, because the right conditions are not present. In this sense, we always need to remember that even the second union is a kind of "state of life", in other words, a permanent situation that has to be modified somehow if the confessor is to recognize in the sinner the conversion required in order to receive sacramental forgiveness. Without a firm and manifest resolution at least not to commit acts of adultery, the sinner cannot be absolved. This is a point that must be considered in any penitential process proposed to these persons.

13. *If mercy is the guiding principle of all pastoral care, why limit it with ecclesiastical laws?*

The **moral law** is a statement of minimum requirements, below which an action is always bad, and therefore this is a limit that helps us not to stray from the path of moral maturation. Because of its inherent objectivity, based on the moral object involved in the concrete actions, this law designates a positive communication of the good with a universal scope. In this sense, the law is not a limit to freedom, but rather an aid to attaining freedom's authentic end: to enable us to love. In this context, thanks to the connection between law, freedom, and love, mercy is completely in harmony with the moral law.

The adequate formulation of moral laws avoids the arbitrariness of someone who would try to impose his will on others, which is always an injustice. In effect it usually happens that the person who does not respect the laws of the authority then wants to impose his own laws on others. The Church helps her faithful to discern their own moral path with her authoritative teaching about what is in keeping with the *natural law*, in compliance with her responsibility to guide Christians to the salvation given by God. On this basis, she proposes ecclesial laws that show us how to respect, in our present circumstances, the moral goods in question.

14. *If mercy consists in healing people's wounds, why not apply it to the divorced?*

Mercy enables us, like the Good Samaritan, to "see with the heart", in other words, to discover the real wounds and to pour on them the genuine oil that can heal them. In this respect it is different from mere compassion, which does not heal. Therefore it is essential to **heal the wounds** of divorced couples. Mercy enables us to see that every divorce is a wound, both for the offending spouse, because he has sinfully failed to live up to a commitment, and for the offended spouse who suffers from the injustice. The romantic view that it is possible to "start over again from zero" if another intense affection appears, causing all the previous ones to vanish and be forgotten, is false. Someone who seeks to enter a new union after divorce makes the wound even deeper because he pretends to conceal it and makes it even more difficult to recognize.

This is why the first thing that mercy obliges us to do is precisely to recognize that we are wounded. From a pastoral perspective, in order to heal a wound it is not enough to change a norm; one cannot suppose that that is enough to resolve the problem. What is necessary instead is a true change of heart, the ability to discover the profound meaning of the gifts received from God. Mercy gives to the offended party the ability to forgive, which is the most divine way of acknowledging the permanence of a bond based on God's forgiveness. The guilty party, thanks to mercy, is healed of his infidelity, so as to be able to remain faithful to the covenant that God sealed with his love, by making whatever changes may be necessary.

Every healing takes time, according to what is described as the **law of gradualness**, given that a person gradually manages to "see with the heart" his utter dependence on mercy. This process requires pastoral accompaniment that is in keeping with this divine standard. It is the opposite of what occurs with the "gradualness of the law", which does not consider the promptings of mercy to conversion and tries to adapt the norm to the supposed abilities of the person, applying a purely human measure without taking grace into account.

IV. Canon Law and Flexibility

15. *If persons are unrepeatable and laws are generic, why not apply* epikeia *to the specific cases of the divorced and remarried?*

Every person is unique, and so are the personal relationships that are essential in order to find one's own identity. These relationships are the bonds of love that every person establishes so as to be able to lead a full life, and that are sustained by the objective character of definite goods. Without faithfulness to these ties, the person loses his moral identity and his path of fulfillment.

The moral law is based on the understanding of the truth of the good that (1) allows persons to communicate objectively and (2) establishes the identity of the personal ties involved in parenthood, childhood, friendship, marriage, cooperation, and solidarity. Without these relational goods, the life of a person is seriously dehumanized.

Epikeia is the virtue of finding exceptions to a law, considering that the legislator's intention was not to apply it to that concrete case despite the wording of the law. We can tell immediately from this explanation that *epikeia* cannot be applied to the natural law, inasmuch as the natural law is universal, while at the same time implying the concrete human act in the context of the communication of the good. Purported exceptions to the natural law imply the idea of an arbitrary God who gives to some and demands from others.

The moral law of marriage is part of the natural law; its universality is obvious inasmuch as it is "based on the nature of the human person and his acts" (*GS* 51). *Epikeia* is not applicable in the case of divorce, because someone who finds himself in that situation and marries another spouse commits adultery in every case. There are no exceptions to "Thou shalt not commit adultery", just are there are none to "Thou shalt not kill."

16. *Why are there so many laws about marriage, which is a matter of love? Might not canon law be contrary to the spirit of pastoral mercy, which is essentially flexible?*

Love as a personal reality is the source of stable bonds that create obligations based on **relations of justice**. This is why, in order to be authentic, love demands respect for justice. Conjugal love is the basis of marriage. It is this love that explains the characteristics proper to marriage as an institution. These characteristics have an objective and universal character, so that they do not depend on the vicissitudes of human affections but on the truth of the good involved.

The canon law of marriage is the expression of the goods of justice pertaining to this institution willed by

God, and it defends these goods. A just law is the way to defend the position of the weaker against the stronger, and this simple fact aligns the law with mercy.

The real defense of these rights is not contrary to flexibility and creativity in conjugal love, which are essential in order to overcome the various problems that can arise and to promote the growth of love itself. This characteristic is described as the *pastoral dimension of canon law.*

17. *What happens when a divorced-and-remarried person thinks in conscience that his first marriage was invalid?*

By its objective and legal nature, marriage as an institution is a social reality. This is why, although the question of the validity of one's marriage is a **matter of conscience**, given that marriage involves the whole person, the issue is not reduced to that, inasmuch as marriage results from an interpersonal relationship that involves another person. Personal conviction that a marriage is invalid cannot be considered as definitive evidence for judging the marriage nonexistent; this conviction must be subjected to the judgment of the competent authorities within the Church.

Overcoming the trend that privatizes marriage, freedom and love is an essential point in understanding this social dimension. This is about the consequences of privatizing conscience, which is interpreted as a solipsistic, purely self-referential judgment that makes its own judgment absolute in comparison with that of any other person.

If someone has serious doubts about the validity of his first marriage, it is necessary to resolve them by consulting experts who can give their valid opinions and by relying on the judgment of the ecclesiastical tribunals of the Church. Far from leaving everything solely to the judgment of the individual conscience, in this way the person is accompanied in an ecclesial discernment, as is fitting for a social (and not merely private) reality such as marriage.

V. The Indissolubility of Marriage: Justice and Mercy

18. *What does it mean for marriage to be a sacrament if it is natural for a man and a woman to join in a stable union so as to start a family?*

In marriage a special **manifestation of God's plan** for mankind occurs, which is revealed and accomplished through the *human love* of a man and a woman. This love is manifested in its unique value, because it is exclusive, permanent, and open to life. In this love man discovers a transcendent presence that far surpasses a mere agreement of will. This dimension of transcendence, which corresponds in a *natural* way to spousal love, is radically open to a deeper revelation of the real presence of the love of God in human love.

The love of God for his people was presented by the prophets as a spousal love in anticipation of a definitive, indestructible New Covenant (see for example Ezek 16), like the one that Jesus achieved through the gift of his body on the Cross so as to unite himself eucharistically to his Church in "one flesh". This is the same covenant that Christian spouses represent and achieve through their own exclusive and indissoluble gift (cf. Eph 5:32). Therefore this is about a gift of God that originates *within* the love that leads them to give themselves to each other, thus confirming in a new dimension the significance of the bond created by natural human love.

To believe in the flesh of Christ (cf. 2 Jn 7) therefore requires that we believe in the **grace of the sacrament** of matrimony as an indissoluble union; we are talking about an expression of grace and not about a problem because of which it is necessary to find exceptions. Probably the secularization of marriage was the worst attack on the very nature of this union. It started with Luther's denial of its sacramental significance and continued with the invention of civil marriage without any transcendent reference—an institution different from and opposed to natural marriage.

19. *How can marriage be indissoluble if love is subject to so many vicissitudes? What meaning does indissolubility have when "love is dead"?*

Marriage is naturally indissoluble because spousal love, the love that spouses promise one another, is directed to the person and to his ability to love and not to his qualities, which can indeed vary. This is why the promise "forever" contains a profound personal meaning that goes beyond emotions and feelings and establishes and ensures a bond between the spouses which, as such, lasts until the death of one of them.

"Romantic love" is the kind that can die, and it does in fact die on many occasions, but this has nothing to do with the permanence of conjugal love, which is the indicator of its truth. It is necessary to heal persons of the weakness of romantic love so that they can discover love as a source in which to regenerate their relationships.

Despite the enormous strength of human love when it is open to transcendence, it is understandable that, because of the weakness of sin and "hardness of heart" (Mt 19:8), situations can arise in which it becomes humanly impossible to continue to live together as love would have it. But precisely in these situations the strength of Christ appears, the power of a "crucified love" (Saint Ignatius of Antioch) that in the baptized person proclaims "Christ ... lives in me" (see Gal 2:20) and makes us sharers in the mercy of his heart, so that "if we are faithless, he remains faithful—for he cannot deny himself" (2 Tim 2:13). This is what we experience in the baptism that remains forever even if we are unfaithful; this is the truth of the irrevocable gift of God's love in us. The love of God remains in the mystery of his gift even when the acts of the person try "to kill it".

When marriage attains its full sacramental significance of **being "one flesh"** (i.e., a ratified and consummated marriage), it shares fully in the gift of God's love and becomes part of the irreversible covenant with God, even when man is unfaithful to this love. He can always count on the gift of grace, which will enable him to live in accordance with the demands of fidelity to this love, thanks to the promise of Christ, who is faithful.

20. *Given an irreversible separation, is it not inhumane to oblige the persons to live alone, without the possibility of "making a new life for themselves"? Could not the ecclesial authority loosen the bond as it does with religious and priests?*

"What therefore God has joined together, let no man put asunder" (Mt 19:6). This is such a daunting demand that the disciples themselves found it excessive: "If such is the case of a man with his wife, it is not expedient to marry" (Mt 19:10). "Only those to whom it is given" (Mt 19:11) understand the profound truth contained in Christ's words. It is the gift of divine mercy that heals the spouses' hardness of heart and makes them capable of living out their marriage in Christ.

This too means **"making a new life for themselves"**, but starting from the truth of their own life, because "whoever ... marries another [wife], commits adultery" (Mt 19:9). It is a question of the "life ... hidden with Christ in God" (Col 3:3), a life in accordance with the gift of grace that shares in Christ's faithfulness despite men's unfaithfulness. This is what makes it possible to practice fidelity in difficult situations, within marriage also, for instance, in the case of prolonged continence because of an illness.

The prohibition of a new union is testimony to a new faithfulness that Christ alone makes possible. Those who remain faithful to their matrimonial bond in the difficult state of irreversible separation from their spouse are eminent witnesses of the truth of God's love in this world. In their situation they need support and recognition from the Christian community so that they may understand that God is not abandoning them to loneliness.

This is a question of the **truth of a sacramental bond** received from Christ; therefore, with regard to the indissolubility of a fully sacramental marriage, the Church has the authority only to administer the sacrament and cannot dissolve "what God has joined together". In contrast, she can dispense from religious vows or priestly promises, which depend on ecclesiastical authority and can be dissolved for serious reasons. This is not the case, however, with the sacrament of Holy Orders, which lasts forever even though the priest is unfaithful to the gift that he has received; even if he apostatizes and loses the faith, he will be "a priest for ever" (Heb 5:6) and the Church will never be able to relieve him of his priesthood.

21. *Why deny Holy Communion to a divorced-and-remarried*
    Catholic who has repented for having broken up his first
    marriage? How can you say that the Church does not
    discriminate against divorced Catholics who live together
    as spouses, given that they are the only ones to whom
    Communion is denied?

The Church has the mission to safeguard the just admin-
istration of the sacraments so that they might be fruitful.
For this reason she has the duty to deny Holy Communion to those who publicly are not correctly disposed to
receive it. Included among these are all those in an irregular public situation, as in the case of divorced persons who
live together with someone other than their spouse. The
Church cannot admit them to Holy Communion until
they change their objectively sinful situation. There is a
close relation between the Eucharist and the matrimonial
bond because of its sacramental significance (see *Sacramentum caritatis*, no. 29).

To receive the Eucharist in a state far removed from
God is no help at all for a sinner, because, as Saint Paul
says, he then "eats and drinks judgment upon himself"
(1 Cor 11:29). Furthermore, this causes scandal for those
who see the incongruity between remaining in an irregular
state of life and approaching Holy Communion. There is an
objective contradiction between the sacramental union of
Christ the Bridegroom with the Church, his Bride, which
is accomplished in the Eucharist, and the unfaithfulness of
the divorced person who is living with another person.

The repentance that is required of a divorced person in
an irregular situation is the same as what is required of any
other penitent: that he renounce not only a sin committed

in the past, but any sin whatsoever that he might commit in the present, such as the **adulterous situation** in which he is living.

The Church **in no way discriminates** in denying Holy Communion to a person who is living in a state contrary to his union with God. Cohabitation outside of the sacrament of matrimony is not the only sinful situation in which this occurs; the Church can give Communion to an apostate only if he publicly professes the faith in its entirety.

The Church, however, does not abandon the sinner who shows signs of repentance, even though it is not yet complete. The Church wants to be close to the sinner, to the point of recommending that he make a spiritual communion—not in the sense of achieving a full union with God, which is impossible as long as the impediment exists, but in the sense of increasing his desire to receive Communion through a penitential journey.

VI. The Testimony of the Church's Tradition

22. *Is it certain that in order to avoid "greater evils", the Council of Nicaea demanded that also the divorced and remarried be admitted to Communion?*

This is not true. The Council says in canon 8: "With respect to those [i.e., the Novatianists] who call themselves 'the Cathars' [the pure ones] ... it is fitting that they profess in writing ... to remain in communion with those who have been married twice and with those who have lapsed during a persecution" (DH 127). When it speaks about "those who have been married twice" (*dígamoi*), the Council is referring to those who are **widowed and remarried**. The meaning of this text is made extremely clear by the context of the canon, which defines the minimum requirements for the reintegration of the Novatians to ecclesial communion, by the specific terminology of the Church Fathers, who never use the word *dígamoi* to refer to an irregular situation, and by the previous and later testimonies stating that forbidding a widowed person to remarry is a Novatian error. There are, in fact, excellent reasons for rejecting the interpretation of Cereti, who claimed to apply the canon to the divorced and remarried by means of a manipulated argument that was deprived of its historical basis. The canon of the Council of Nicaea provides no support for a pastoral approach of tolerance with the divorced and remarried.

23. *Why does Origen consider tolerance of a second marriage for divorced persons "not unreasonable"?*

In a passage from his *Commentary on the Gospel of Saint Matthew* (14, 23), Origen speaks of the tolerance of "some leaders of the Church" in permitting a second marriage for a divorced woman whose husband was alive. Three times he states that this is "contrary to the original law reported by the *Scripture*" (emphasis added) and hence passes on this incident a *negative* judgment coming from the highest authority. Once he has established this point, he discusses the reason for the abuse and says: "They did not act in a way that was entirely without reason", which is different from simply being "not unreasonable". There are reasons: to avoid "greater evils", although this point is clearly inadequate in comparison to the authority of *Sacred Scripture*. The presentation by the Alexandrian theologian shows how the Church Fathers consider human reasons, that is, what we would call extenuating circumstances, in light of the higher authority of Scripture, which is why the fundamental judgment is negative. Origen's position can by no means be considered evidence for a sort of tolerance; on the contrary, it is an argument against it. According to Origen, this is, in fact, a practice that goes beyond what is licit.

24. *Do the number and the importance of patristic texts that testify to a sort of tolerance with the divorced and remarried oblige us to revise the current discipline of the Church, which appears to be too rigid?*

In reality there are few patristic texts that testify to a sort of tolerance with the divorced and remarried (no more than ten), and every one of them is obscure. Generally speaking, they refer to very specific cases that have been extrapolated from unclear allusions; more context would be needed in order to understand their full significance. This is a minimal number of passages, in comparison with the numerous texts that speak about a discipline that regards those who remarry while their spouse is still alive as adulterers and does not admit them to Communion unless they change their way of life. The intention is to offer a specifically **Christian praxis different** from that of Roman law and of the pagan world in general. We are talking about a fundamental question for the Christian believer and a very necessary witness in the present moment.

Taken as a whole, at most these texts require some clarification of the sources, but in no way do they testify "that in the early church there was, according to customary law in many local churches, the praxis of pastoral tolerance, clemency, and forbearance" (*Gospel of the Family*, p. 37). That assertion is totally unfounded. The passages in question express, rather, the need to resolve legally, in keeping with the truth of Scripture, the more difficult cases that required some clarification. The juridical value of marriage is very clear at this stage of Church history.

In conclusion, these texts, by themselves, do not have the doctrinal weight necessary to consider a change in the present discipline of the Catholic Church.

25. *Does the practice of* oikonomia *in the Orthodox Church originate with the Church Fathers?*

It is necessary to distinguish the concept of **Orthodox oikonomia** from the application thereof to the case of the remarriage of divorced persons. There is an entirely valid theological concept of *oikonomia* having a patristic basis: it consists in looking at the value of pastoral actions in the overall divine plan that develops progressively as a discernment in wisdom. This is an altogether fruitful perspective for the Catholic Church.

The practice of legally allowing the remarriage of divorced persons, in contrast, originated in Byzantium because legislation by the Byzantine emperors was imposed on the ecclesial discipline—in other words, because the temporal power prevailed upon the life of the Church. This is a typical case of Caesaro-papism, which has no foundation whatsoever in the Church Fathers and is contrary to anything envisaged by the Gospel.

It is wrong to think that Orthodox *oikonomia* is closer to the primitive Church, with regard to the divorced and remarried, while the discipline of the Latin Church is supposedly a rigid and late type of Augustinianism. In reality, the main support for a clarification of the real value of the matrimonial bond was precisely the great dogmatic development concerning the sacraments that was accomplished in early Scholasticism; this helped to elaborate even more clearly the fundamentals of the current practice of the Latin Church.

In fact, the Latin Church never accepted the Greek practice. Although at the Council of Trent, where the validity of the current practice of the Church was declared explicitly, the Orthodox position was not entirely rejected, presently a retraction is required in order to be admitted to Catholic communion.

26. *What should we think about the pastoral flexibility of the Orthodox, who allow a second marriage after a suitable penitential period?*

The pastoral flexibility of the Orthodox, who allow a second marriage after a penitential period, should be considered as **the abuse of a civil authority** which, for reasons basically of political convenience, demanded its acceptance on the part of the Orthodox churches. This is why there is a wide variety of practices and various legislation in this regard. In many cases it became a mere dispensation. A fee is paid so that the local bishop, without any in-depth examination of the reasons for the petition and for the spouses' situation, might give permission for a second or a third marriage.

The penitential practice proposed in these churches presupposes from the outset an acceptance of the second marriage, and therefore there is no discernment as to the truth of the situation of the contracting parties. The practice goes to show that the second marriage does not have the same sacramental value as the first, in other words, that there are first-class Christians and second-class Christians. It is very difficult to accept this fact as part of the truth of the definitive *oikonomia* that Christ inaugurated by his grace, inasmuch as it is definitive and we cannot expect any other.

Only a tendentious and spiritualized presentation of this practice can make it appear like a model for Catholics to follow; in reality this is a clear example of the fact that, if the door is opened to little exceptions, you always end up following a completely liberal praxis.

VII. Pastoral Benevolence in Specific Situations

27. *Why not allow pastoral kindness that sees in specific cases sufficient reasons not to apply a doctrinal law that is too strict? Might not the current rigidity be one reason why many people leave the Church and others disparage Christianity? Is it possible that many people would come to the Church if she changed her discipline?*

Ultimately, the question about admitting divorced-and-remarried persons to Holy Communion is not an argument on which you can find an intermediate position between a rigorist and a laxist pastoral approach. It is about recognizing a question of justice due to **weighty doctrinal reasons**, specifically the real and absolute indissolubility of a ratified and consummated marriage. To try to conceal these reasons is an example of what Benedict XVI described as "**pseudo-pastoral claims** that would situate questions on a purely horizontal plane, on which what matters is to satisfy subjective requests" (Address to the Roman Rota, January 29, 2010).

The truth may seem rigid if it is considered in a way extrinsic to one's own desires. The curative pastoral task has to do precisely with these desires—as Jesus did in speaking with the Samaritan woman (see Jn 4:1–45): first of all he awakened her desire for the gift of God, then he made her confront the reality of her life, and finally he showed her the way of conversion to the faith. The gift of God does, in fact, have an absolute meaning that comes into conflict with the current environment of relativism. For someone who considers everything relative, any truth will be a sign of rigidity.

The experience of the non-Catholic Christian communities that have integrated moral relativism into their ecclesial practices shows beyond all doubt that this decision, far from attracting people, distances them even more from Christian life, which no longer has any special force for them or any human grandeur that could make it attractive.

This is why the *sensus fidelium* of Christians at the moment of believing—of which Cardinal Newman spoke and which was taken up by the Second Vatican Council [*Lumen gentium*, nos. 12 and 35]—must never be confused with a meaningless opinion poll about moral questions. The latter always involves a least-common-denominator approach that necessarily implies some form of relativism. Max Weber clearly demonstrated this with his theory of ethical polytheism. The life of holy spouses, in contrast, shines as a real witness to the life of faith in the midst of this world.

28. *What path of conversion can be proposed to the divorced and remarried? Are there any positive proposals?*

The Church expresses her mercy toward the divorced and remarried by her closeness to them and by **proposing a true path of conversion** and accompanying them on it. The purpose of this process is true healing of the wounds resulting from their situation. Indeed, such programs already exist in many places, and there is also a real interest in seeing them implemented.

The first step is always the recognition in an ecclesial, communal setting of the truth of one's own situation in God's sight. The divorced and remarried must acknowledge their own possible responsibility for the breakup, the fact that one of their decisions put them in a sinful situation, inasmuch as they were unfaithful to their earlier promise. They must acknowledge the need to repair all the damage that has resulted from it, in particular with respect to their children. They must acknowledge the permanence of the bond and the need for fidelity to it, as well as the need to live in the Church according to the Gospel so as to continue their journey. This is a process that must be communal and at the same time personalized.

The major difficulty is the fact that within the Church this type of accompaniment is extremely rare. Such programs would be necessary, for example, also for couples experiencing problems and for separated couples who want to be faithful to their marriage, but attention to these very serious problems is almost nonexistent. In particular one finds an almost total abandonment of married couples during the first years of marriage, precisely in the years when more than 50 percent of separations occur.

29. *As an exception, would it not perhaps be a good witness for the children if parents in an irregular situation were allowed to receive Communion?*

The primary victims of separations and divorces are the children, who want more than anything else for their parents to love each other, which is the greatest good that parents can give their children. The emotional privation of the children is aggravated by divorce, because the situation becomes very difficult to reverse.

Sooner or later the children will have to know what the true situation of their parents is. Accepting this situation is something much more complex than mere admission to Communion. To think otherwise is another example of a pastoral approach based more on one's own subjective desires than on fulfilling God's plan for the persons involved and on the conversion that it presupposes. The testimony of the truth can never be relegated to a secondary position, even if that means no longer going to Communion when one is conscious of being unable to do so. Otherwise the children would come to think it were possible to separate Eucharistic Communion from life, and that would end up jeopardizing their faith or making it irrelevant.

30. *Given the importance of the situation of the divorced and remarried, why not concentrate the Synod on this topic?*

Dealing with one category of the sick while excluding others is never a good practice. It would be even worse if, in the case of an epidemic, a decision was made to treat only a specific strain, while ignoring the fact that the **epidemic** has many different manifestations. Indeed, divorce is only one of the many difficulties that arise for an emo-tivist subject who lives in a sex-driven culture.

It is part of a legalistic mindset to think that if a norm is changed and we become more flexible about an irregular situation, the problem will disappear. Cases concerned with marriage and family are due to a widespread malady that produces many sick people. Treating only one case while excluding the others just runs the risk of aggravating them all.

We started with the observation that we are facing a major cultural challenge caused by the loss of the meaning of conjugal love in the life of persons. For the Church to take a step toward implicit acceptance of this fact would be a kind of **cultural suicide** that would make the gospel of marriage and the family irrelevant.

INDEX

absolution, 157n68, 161–62, 223–24

abstinence
   health problems associated with, 25–26, 33
   premarital, 145–46
   for remarried and divorced couples, 38–43

"accompaniment", pastoral approach as, 164–67, 199–200, 217, 226, 241

"adequate anthropology", 17, 215

adolescent mentality, 217–18

adultery, 87–88, 156–58, 223–24, 227, 233–34. *See also* divorced couples; remarried couples

affective education, 216

"affective illiteracy", 216

agreements, prenuptial, 134–35

aman, etymology of, 65

analysis, criteria for text, 98–101

Anatrella, Tony, 52

Anglican churches, "assisted religious suicide" of, 44–45. *See also* Christianity

annulment process, marriage, 34–35, 128–29

"anthropology, adequate", 17, 215

Arendt, Hannah, 126n4, 132–33

assisted religious suicide, 44–45

"atomism, chronological", 140

Augustine of Hippo, 47–48, 111–12, 121–22

baptism, of divorced catechumen, 121–22

Basil, canon of, 117–19

Bauman, Zygmunt, 131–32

Beauvoir, Simone de, 52

Benedict XVI (pope). *See also* Ratzinger, Joseph
   on application of epikeia, 193
   on faith as burden, 138n28
   on marriage and faith, 170–71
   on monogamous marriage, 68
   on seeking exceptions, 180–84

bigamy, 30–31, 112

blended families, 36–37

Blondel, Maurice, 148–49

Bond
   basic human relationships as personal, 173, 226,
   as consumer good, 133
   covenant with God as, 64, 70, 76
   as created in sexual encounters, 144
   of justice, 174
   love as source of, 227, 229
   of marriage, 28, 38, 70, 87, 94, 210, 218, 232, 233, 238
      the breaking of through death, 92
      as conditional, 135
      as dispensed from by ecclesial authority, 231, 232
      ecclesial understanding of, 95, 96